Lincoln Kirstein: A First Bibliography

Portraits by Lachaise, Noguchi and Tchelitchew
Photograph by Richard Benson

LINCOLN KIRSTEIN

THE PUBLISHED WRITINGS

1922—1977

A FIRST BIBLIOGRAPHY

COMPILED BY HARVEY SIMMONDS
LOUIS H. SILVERSTEIN
NANCY LASSALLE

NEW HAVEN
YALE UNIVERSITY LIBRARY
1978

TABLE OF CONTENTS

FOREWORD *by A. Hyatt Mayor*   9

INTRODUCTION   11

CHRONOLOGY   17

PHOTOGRAPHS   33

THE BIBLIOGRAPHY   41

FICTION   43
Books   45
In Periodicals   45

POETRY   47
Books and Pamphlets   50
In Books and Periodicals   50

DRAMA AND BALLET LIBRETTI   55
Full-length Plays   57
Ballet Libretti   57

ON DANCE   61
Books   63
In Books   66
Articles and Reviews   68
Program and Other Notes   80
Exhibition Catalogues and Notes   86

ON DRAWING, PAINTING, SCULPTURE, AND ARCHITECTURE   89
Books   91
In Books   91
Articles and Reviews   92
Museum and Gallery Catalogues and Notes   100

ON PHOTOGRAPHY   107
   In Books   109
   Articles and Reviews   110
   Exhibition Notes   111

ON FILM   113
   Articles and Reviews   115

ON MUSIC AND DRAMA   119
   In Books   121
   Articles and Reviews   121
   Program and Other Notes 123

ON LITERATURE, HISTORY, POLITICS,
AND OTHER SUBJECTS   125
   In Books   127
   Articles and Reviews   127

INDEX   139

FOREWORD

I MIGHT attempt a biography of Proteus, but Lincoln Kirstein? Whatever he animates, he is basically a poet in the Greek sense of a maker and shaper. He not only writes his poems, he makes them happen. *Hound & Horn* was his first concrete poem. Another was the revival of Rimmer, and of Nadelman, while his most conspicuous poem is the New York City Ballet and its School, which he dreamed in secret long before America showed any sense of the dance, and of dancers who are forever young, forever energized by being immolated in a regal discipline. When he brought ballet to this country the transplanting generated as much energy as transplanting had done when theatrical dancing came long ago to an innocent and innovative Russia.

What have we that can transmit the brusque vibrancy of his voice, his energy, his authority? We have his writings. The writings store up and breathe the impact of his presence. The difference Lincoln has made in American awareness is history.

A. HYATT MAYOR

INTRODUCTION

DURING every generation a few exceptional individuals appear who are incisively dedicated and destined to the achievement of unique missions in the art of their time. The best of these persons seem to burn like beacons of supreme consciousness or conscience during the lifetime they inhabit. Implacable and original in overcoming obstacles in their fidelity to a vision, even before the responsibility of their accomplishments becomes fully known the leadership provided may be recognized as the making of legend.

Lincoln Kirstein has been known to the general public primarily as General Director, founder, supporter, and collaborator with George Balanchine since 1934 in the establishment and maintenance of the School of American Ballet, and the New York City Ballet which for more than twenty-five years has been the leading company in the creation and performance of original works based on classic ballet technique and native vernacular dance. A theatrical producer who has operated as a public benefactor, he is the instigator and supporter of an untold number of dance, theater, exhibition, and publication projects. On behalf of art forms, artists and works of art, he has invented schools, companies, exhibits, and repertories, and has stimulated means to sustain them.

While it is far too early to assess the career and work of Lincoln Kirstein, this first bibliography of his published writings to date, accompanied by a chronology, is an initial step. An author who continues to publish widely, his writings form an important body of work in themselves. Together, his books, articles and essays have functioned to support and illuminate the central meaning of his enterprises. They include a continuing assessment and appreciation of the accomplishments of individual artists and creators, many of whom became friends and collaborators. The writings chronicle an attitude of full responsibility. In them the author performs the role of poet, novelist, historian, essayist, scholar, and critic—even more, and perhaps essentially, the role of the artist acting in the guise of being a member of the audience, by active appreciation making possible works of art and performances that would not otherwise exist.

Throughout the contents of this bibliography a unifying point of view is evident. The point of view is at once intellectual and civil, esthetic and practical, democratic and aristocratic, effectively complex without being paradoxical. It is marked by a determination to serve art and the public, championing by actual example in performance rather than by theory, claim or ulterior motivation.

The writings act to perpetuate especially those historic forms of art which are based on or depict the inexhaustible grace and vitality of the human body, schooled and trained as instrument and subject in art. They study the human image given formal expression, particularly in dance and the visual arts, whether still (as in sculpture and photographs) or in motion (as in dance and on film). The author's efforts may be said to have helped not only to renew classic ballet so that it has taken root in the United States as a native art form, but also to reassert classic human values and formality in other arts. The writings develop values superficially renounced during an age ravaged by fragmentation and exploitation. They oppose the new philistinism that battens on technological excuse. They battle on behalf of the employment of the inherited techniques of discipline most modern esthetics have assiduously sought to abandon. One finds in the writings explicit conviction that authentic modernity in art arises from spontaneous progression, not from a programmatic rejection of the past.

The author's principal identifications have been with such compeers and associates as Balanchine, Stravinsky, T. S. Eliot, W. H. Auden, E. M. Forster, Eisenstein, Tchelitchew, Walker Evans, Hart Crane, James Agee, and Henri Cartier-Bresson. Also evident are particular interest in and influences by American artists and exemplars for whom art and life were co-equal or closely related forms of public performance, the public mask being correlated to a deeply private self: figures such as Walt Whitman, Abraham Lincoln and Thomas Eakins, and others of European origin, notably Diaghilev, Nijinsky and Nadelman.

The bibliography is based on standard indexes and available primary sources, composed of an unusually broad range of periodicals, books, exhibition catalogues, programs, and newspapers. The independent and pioneering nature of Lincoln Kirstein's interests has resulted in appearances not only in established and easily located publications, but as well in some now obscure and difficult to trace. In certain categories, such as program and exhibition notes, letters to newspapers and periodicals, and occasional writings, the entries depend on random scrapbooks, clipping files, and incomplete archival collections. As this is a first bibliography and chronology, the compilers will gratefully receive any additional information.

The unorthodoxy of the career allows for unusual presentation. The bibliography is divided into two major categories: first, the published writings in creative forms—fiction, poetry, drama, and ballet libretti; and second, books, essays, reviews, commentaries, and notes on dance; on drawing, painting, sculpture, and architecture; on photography; on film; on music and drama; and on literature, history, politics, and other subjects. Citations are arranged chronologically under each heading. The consistency is evident throughout: an essay in 1975 carries forward ideas formulated clearly in 1932 or earlier. One or more books or major statements in each field of interest have followed previous writings which were preparatory explorations. Each section of the bibliography is preceded by a representative excerpt from the author's published work.

At the time of this compilation Lincoln Kirstein has published twenty books. Twelve are on dance, two are novels, two are volumes of poetry, two are on drawing, two are on sculpture. In the listing of books in the bibliography, distinct editions are noted but not later printings by the original publishers. Those items not seen by the compilers appear fully enclosed in brackets.

The listings of contributions by Lincoln Kirstein under the titles of periodicals he founded and edited do not indicate his editorial guidance and responsibility for their continued existence. These include the distinguished literary journal *Hound & Horn* (1927–1934); *Films* (1939–1940); and *Dance Index* (1942–1948). Entries in the bibliography titled "Comment" served as prefaces to issues on special subjects often conceived and edited by him.

Many of the articles and books include sections of photographs and illustrations the author selected and arranged. These are essential to the texts and are in themselves significant to a degree not possible to make clear in the abbreviated citations of this volume.

Lincoln Kirstein's numerous unsigned notes on ballets in the programs of the American Ballet Company, Ballet Caravan, American Ballet Caravan, Ballet Society, and since 1948, the New York City Ballet, have not been listed. Archival files may be consulted in the Dance Collection of The New York Public Library.

The author is known to have a number of writing projects in progress and further publications have been announced. The writings cited are those completed prior to May 4, 1977. There exists in addition a large body of completed but unpublished work.

Introduction

In the course of compiling this bibliography a collection of excerpts from many of the less accessible items has been made; typescripts of these excerpts are on deposit at the Yale University Library and at the Dance Collection of The New York Public Library.

The compilers are grateful to the staffs of the Dance Collection and Research Libraries of The New York Public Library, the Boston Public Library, the Library of the Museum of Modern Art, the Columbia University Library, the Harvard University Library, the Sterling and Beinecke Libraries of Yale University, and to the particular individuals who have assisted in making the publication possible.

Public tributes to artists, friends and associates appear frequently among the author's writings. It is appropriate that this bibliography has been prepared as a tribute to Lincoln Kirstein. This publication of the Yale University Library is a gift to him from George Balanchine, Mina Curtiss, Ira M. Danburg, Philip Johnson, George G. Kirstein, W. McNeil Lowry, Nelson A. Rockefeller, Mrs. Igor Stravinsky, Monroe Wheeler, the Committee for the Dance Collection of The New York Public Library, the Dance Theatre of Harlem, the Eakins Press Foundation, the Ford Foundation, the Lassalle Fund, the New York City Ballet, and the School of American Ballet.

LESLIE GEORGE KATZ

NANCY LASSALLE

HARVEY SIMMONDS

CHRONOLOGY

1907 MAY 4

Lincoln Edward Kirstein is born in Rochester, New York, second of the three children (Mina Stein Kirstein Curtiss, George Garland Kirstein) of Louis Edward and Rose (Stein) Kirstein; named after Abraham Lincoln.

1912

The Kirstein family moves to Boston.

1920 APRIL

With his cousin Nathaniel Woolf attends ballet for the first time, seeing Pavlova's Boston performances.

1921 JUNE

Completes his elementary education at the Edward Devotion School, Brookline, Massachusetts.

1921 FALL—SPRING 1922

Attends Phillips Exeter Academy, where he meets James Agee. First publication, "The Silver Fan" (a play set in Tibet), in the *Phillips Exeter Monthly*.

1922

First of regular summer visits to London and the Continent. In this and subsequent summers meets Maynard Keynes, E. M. Forster, others of the Bloomsbury circle, and the Sitwells; attends the London seasons of Diaghilev's Ballets Russes.

1922 FALL—SPRING 1924

Attends the Berkshire School, Sheffield, Massachusetts, where he meets George Platt Lynes.

1924 SUMMER

Meets G. I. Gurdgieff in Fontainebleau.

1925

Works in the Boston stained-glass factory of Charles J. Connick.

1926 FALL

Enters Harvard University; studies under S. Foster Damon, humanist and Blake scholar; is awarded a prize for freehand drawing.

1926 WINTER

Becomes active in New York. Meets Muriel Draper, Carl Van Vechten, and others.

1927 SEPTEMBER

First issue of *Hound & Horn*, the quarterly which he founded with Varian Fry, of which he was editor with R. P. Blackmur, Bernard Bandler, A. Hyatt Mayor, Allen Tate, and Yvor Winters, and to which he contributed articles on dance, art, literature, and other subjects until its final issue in 1934. Among other contributors were Ezra Pound, T. S. Eliot, Katherine Anne Porter, James Agee, Michael Gold, Granville Hicks, Glenway Wescott, Harry Crosby, Irving Babbitt, Edmund Wilson, and E. E. Cummings.

1928 DECEMBER

With classmates John Walker III and Edward M. M. Warburg founds the Harvard Society for Contemporary Art, a precursor of New York's Museum of Modern Art. Among exhibitions were "School of Paris," "Modern German Presses," "Modern Mexican Art," "American Folk Painting," "International Photography," "The Bauhaus," Ben Shahn, Alexander Calder,

Buckminster Fuller, Derain, Matisse, Picasso, and Despiau.

1929

Studies abroad in preparation for his Harvard dissertation on El Greco. Sees first Balanchine ballet, *Prodigal Son*, at a performance of the Diaghilev Ballets Russes. Is present by chance at Diaghilev's funeral in Venice.

1930 JUNE

Is graduated from Harvard University.

1930s

Meets Walker Evans, Hart Crane, W. H. Auden, Ben Shahn, and others; shares a Hudson River summer house at Sneedens Landing with Archibald MacLeish.

1931

Moves to New York City.

1932

Meets Sergei Eisenstein and entertains him in New York.

1932

Publishes first novel, *Flesh Is Heir*, which includes a description of Balanchine's *Prodigal Son* and the funeral of Diaghilev.

1932

Writes the catalogue introduction for the Museum of Modern Art exhibition he initiated and supervised, *Murals by American Painters and Photographers*.

1932

Begins association with Michel Fokine which leads to the publication of *Fokine* (1934); meets Romola Nijinsky and begins work which leads to the publication of *Nijinsky* (1933).

1933–1934

Corresponds with T. E. Lawrence, who becomes the central figure in an unpublished novel.

1933 SUMMER

Lives in Paris and meets Virgil Thomson. Taken to Pavel Tchelitchew's studio by Monroe Wheeler. Through Romola Nijinsky arranges to meet George Balanchine in London; invites Balanchine to come to America to establish a ballet school.

1933 OCTOBER

Arrival of George Balanchine in New York; first efforts, with Lincoln Kirstein, Edward M. M. Warburg and Vladimir Dimitriew, to found a ballet school and company at the Wadsworth Atheneum in Hartford with the assistance of A. Everett Austin, Jr.

1934 JANUARY

The School of American Ballet opens at 637 Madison Avenue, New York City: George Balanchine, Artistic Director and Maître de Ballet; Lincoln Kirstein, Secretary-Treasurer and Director of the Division of Theatrical Sciences.

1934 JUNE

Demonstration debut of the Producing Company of the School of American Ballet at the Warburg estate, White Plains, New York; premiere of first ballet choreographed by Balanchine in the United States, *Serenade*, to music of Peter Ilyich Tchaikovsky.

1934 DECEMBER 6

Premiere of *Transcendence*, first of a number of ballets

with libretti by Lincoln Kirstein, by the Producing Company of the School of American Ballet: Avery Memorial Theater, Hartford, Connecticut.

1935

Publication of *Dance: A Short History of Classical Theatrical Dancing*, and *Low Ceiling*, first book of poems.

1935

After obtaining patronage and commissions for Gaston Lachaise, arranges for a Museum of Modern Art retrospective exhibition of the sculptor's work, and writes the accompanying catalogue.

1935 MARCH

First season of the American Ballet Company, founded by George Balanchine and Lincoln Kirstein: Adelphi Theater, New York City.

1935 OCTOBER

First American Ballet Company tour.

1935 FALL–SPRING 1938

The American Ballet Company provides the ballets for the Metropolitan Opera Association, and performs independently at the Metropolitan Opera House.

1936 SPRING

Organizes Ballet Caravan, a touring company of dancers from the American Ballet Company, with the intention of building a repertory of American work. First performance: Bennington College, July 17; continuing tours through 1941. Commissions include music by Elliott Carter, Paul Bowles, Robert McBride, Virgil Thomson, Aaron Copland, and Henry Brant; choreographers include Lew Christensen, Erick Hawkins, William Dollar, and Eugene Loring.

1936 AUGUST

Stages the dances for Lawrence Langner's production of Molière's *The Would-be Gentleman* with Jimmy Savo and Ruth Weston at the Country Playhouse, Westport, Connecticut, danced by members of Ballet Caravan.

1936 DECEMBER

Appointed head of the Work Projects Administration Federal Dance Theater; through Walker Evans' introduction discusses arts programs with Harry L. Hopkins, administrator of the WPA.

1937 APRIL

American Ballet Company Stravinsky Festival, in close association with the composer, including premiere of *Jeu de Cartes*, commissioned by Lincoln Kirstein and George Balanchine: Metropolitan Opera House.

1938

Arranges the first major exhibition of Walker Evans' photographs at the Museum of Modern Art and writes the text for *Walker Evans: American Photographs*.

1938

Ballet Caravan tour to Havana.

1938 OCTOBER 16

Ballet Caravan premiere of *Billy the Kid*, libretto by Lincoln Kirstein, choreography by Eugene Loring to music commissioned for the ballet from Aaron Copland: Chicago Civic Theater.

1939

Joins Jay Leyda, Mary Losey, Robert Stebbins, and Lee Strasberg in founding the journal *Films*.

1939

Publication of *Ballet Alphabet: A Primer for Laymen*, with drawings by Paul Cadmus.

1939 MAY

The American Ballet Company participates in the first season of the American Lyric Theatre, New York City.

1940

Presents his collection of more than five thousand books and documents on dance to the Museum of Modern Art to form the nucleus of an American archives of the dance; later transferred to the Dance Collection of The New York Public Library.

1940

At the suggestion of Walter Dorwin Teague produces *A Thousand Times Neigh!* for the Ford Motor Company at the New York World's Fair, performed by the dancers of Ballet Caravan for six months and thought to have been seen by a million persons.

1941 APRIL

Marries Fidelma Cadmus.

1941–1943

Consultant to the Museum of Modern Art on Latin-American art; travels in South America to purchase painting and sculpture in 1942; writes the catalogue for the exhibition *The Latin American Collection of the Museum of Modern Art* in 1943.

1941

American Ballet Caravan (the combined American Ballet Company and Ballet Caravan) tours Latin America under the aegis of the United States Office for Coordination of Commercial and Cultural Relations Between the American Republics, through the agency of Nelson A. Rockefeller, Co-ordinator of Inter-American Affairs. In Argentina meets Rosa María Oliver and Victoria Ocampo, principal forces in bringing international culture to South America.

1942

Founds the magazine *Dance Index* with Baird Hastings and Paul Magriel; is one of its editors and a principal contributor through the final issue in 1948; engages Donald Windham as editor 1943–1945, and Marian Eames as managing editor 1946–1948.

1943

Publication of the novel *For My Brother*, based on a Mexican sojourn.

1943

Joins the United States Army; while stationed at Fort Belvoir with the Corps of Engineers studies the history of American battle art.

1944

Publication of *American Battle Painting: 1776–1918*, catalogue of the exhibition shown at the National Gallery of Art in Washington, and the Museum of Modern Art.

1944–1945

Overseas duty in England, France and Germany, including a period as chauffeur to General George S. Patton.

1945 MAY

With Captain Robert K. Posey, Monuments, Fine Arts and Archives Officer, Third United States Army, discovers (in the Steinberg Salt Mine at Alt Aussee) and supervises the recovery of the massive collection of art looted by the Nazis, intended for Hitler's proposed Führer Museum in Linz; later decorated by the Government of the Netherlands for his service.

1945 FALL

Honorable Discharge from the Army, Private First Class.

1946

Publication of *William Rimmer*, catalogue of the exhibition arranged by the author for the Whitney Museum and the Boston Museum of Fine Arts.

1946 FALL

With George Balanchine forms Ballet Society, Inc., a subscription-supported association to further lyric theater in America.

1946 NOVEMBER 20

First Ballet Society performance: Central High School of Needle Trades, New York City. American premiere of Ravel's *The Spellbound Child* with choreography by George Balanchine; premiere of *The Four Temperaments*, Balanchine's ballet to music commissioned by him and Lincoln Kirstein from Paul Hindemith in 1940. Season includes performances of Gian-Carlo Menotti's *The Medium*, and *The Telephone* (commissioned by Ballet Society).

1947

Following the death of Elie Nadelman meets Mrs. Nadelman, and with Mrs. Kirstein moves to Alderbrook, the sculptor's Riverdale home, in order to continue efforts begun while at Harvard to encourage appreciation of the sculptor's work.

1947

Publication of *Pavel Tchelitchew Drawings*.

1947

Ballet Society spring season includes ballets to music commissioned from Elliott Carter, Rudi Revil, Stanley Bate, and John Cage, choreographed by John Taras, Todd Bolender, William Dollar, and Merce Cunningham, with decors by Joan Junyer, Esteban Francés and

Isamu Noguchi. The fall-winter season is held in part at the City Center of Music and Drama, Inc.

1948 APRIL 28
Premiere of *Orpheus*, Balanchine's ballet to music commissioned from Stravinsky by Ballet Society: City Center.

1948 MAY
Morton Baum, Chairman of the Executive Committee of the City Center, invites Ballet Society to become a resident company of the City Center as the New York City Ballet, with Lincoln Kirstein as General Director and George Balanchine as Artistic Director.

1948
Arranges retrospective exhibition of Elie Nadelman's work at the Museum of Modern Art, the Boston Institute of Contemporary Art and the Baltimore Museum of Art; writes the catalogue, *The Sculpture of Elie Nadelman*.

1949–1951
Art critic for the *New Republic*.

1950
First New York City Ballet overseas tour, to England.

1952
Purchases permanent home near Gramercy Park, New York City.

1952
Becomes a member of the Board of Directors of the City Center in May; on October 1 is named Managing Director.

1952
New York City Ballet European tour to Barcelona, The Hague, London, Edinburgh.

1953 JANUARY

Receives the Capezio Award for distinguished service to American dance.

1954

Named advisor to the State Department on American National Theatre and Academy (ANTA) foreign tours.

FROM **1955**

Involved in the planning of Lincoln Center for the Performing Arts.

1955 SUMMER

First season of the American Shakespeare Festival Theatre Academy at Stratford, Connecticut, of which Lincoln Kirstein was a founder and officer, and for which he produced *A Midsummer Night's Dream*.

1956

The School of American Ballet moves to 2291 Broadway.

1956

New York City Ballet tour to Europe.

1957

Receives the American Guild of Musical Artists (AGMA) Award for his service and devotion to the cause of the American dancer.

1957 DECEMBER 1

Premiere of *Agon*, Balanchine's ballet to music commissioned by him and Lincoln Kirstein from Stravinsky.

1958

With the Rockefeller Foundation commissions the opera *Panfilo and Lauretta* from Carlos Chavez and Chester Kallman.

1958

New York City Ballet tour to Japan and Australia.

1958

Lives in Japan for the first of several periods.

1958

Receives the Distinguished Service Award of the National Institute of Arts and Letters.

1958 DECEMBER 4

First performance of the revival of the Weill/Brecht *Seven Deadly Sins* with Lotte Lenya, who appeared in Balanchine's original production for Les Ballets 1933; translation commissioned by Lincoln Kirstein from W. H. Auden and Chester Kallman.

1959

The Division of the Humanities and the Arts of the Ford Foundation, under the leadership of W. McNeil Lowry, Vice President of the Foundation, provides a grant to Ballet Society for a survey of the teaching of ballet in America; subsequent grants to the School of American Ballet make possible a reduced and more selective student body, with scholarship assistance allowing gifted dancers from throughout the country to attend the School.

1959

With the support of Dag Hammarskjöld invites Gagaku, the musicians and dancers of the Japanese Imperial Household, to appear during the New York City Ballet season.

1959

Produces *The Play of Daniel* with Noah Greenberg's Pro Musica Antiqua in the Romanesque Court of The Cloisters, New York City.

1960s

Is active in and becomes an officer of the American Dressage Institute, Saratoga Springs, New York.

1960

Arranges the American tour of the Japanese Grand Kabuki.

1960 SEPTEMBER 27

Awarded the Order of the Sacred Treasure, Fourth Class, by the Japanese Government, for his outstanding contribution to the cultural exchange between the two nations.

1961

Appointed a member of the Advisory Committee on the Arts by President John F. Kennedy.

1961 OCTOBER 4

Produces a Shakespeare Evening in the East Room of the White House following a state dinner for President Ibraham Aboud of the Sudan.

1962

Commissioned by the Seattle World's Fair to arrange a demonstration of traditional Japanese ritual sports; New York City Ballet performs at the Fair.

1962

First New York City Ballet tour to the Soviet Union; series of visits with Sergei Eisenstein's widow, Pera Atasheva.

1962 DECEMBER

Honored by New York City for distinguished and exceptional service following the tour to the Soviet Union.

1963

First of continuing grants to the New York City Ballet

from the Division of the Humanities and the Arts of the Ford Foundation.

1963

Appointed a member of the Citizens Advisory Committee to the Office of Cultural Affairs of the City of New York by Mayor Robert F. Wagner.

1964 APRIL

The New York City Ballet takes up permanent residence at Lincoln Center for the Performing Arts and opens the New York State Theater, designed by Philip Johnson working closely with George Balanchine and Lincoln Kirstein. For the Grand Promenade Lincoln Kirstein arranges the installation of monumental figures carved after small original sculptures by Elie Nadelman.

1964

Publication of *Rhymes of a PFC*, republished in an expanded edition as *Rhymes and More Rhymes of a PFC* in 1966.

1964

Publication of *Pavel Tchelitchew*, catalogue of the exhibition shown at the Gallery of Modern Art, New York City.

1965

Takes part in the Alabama civil rights marches.

1965

New York City Ballet tour to Europe, Israel and England.

1966 JULY

First of continuing seasons at the newly founded Saratoga Performing Arts Center, Saratoga Springs, New York, which is designed in close consultation with the New York City Ballet.

1967

Elected a Benefactor of the Metropolitan Museum of Art.

1967 AUGUST

Production of *White House Happening*, a play about Abraham Lincoln, at the Loeb Drama Center, Harvard University.

1968 JANUARY

Reading of *Magic Carpet*, a play based on Gurdgieffian teaching, at the Harvard Dramatic Club.

1968

Encourages and provides continuing support for the Dance Theatre of Harlem which debuts in 1971, founded and directed by Arthur Mitchell, formerly a principal dancer with the New York City Ballet.

1969

The School of American Ballet moves into specially designed quarters in the new building of the Juilliard School at Lincoln Center.

1969

Elected a Fellow of the American Academy of Arts and Sciences.

1972 JUNE 18–25

The Stravinsky Festival of the New York City Ballet: New York State Theater. The thirty ballets in seven performances include twenty premieres by choreographers George Balanchine, Jerome Robbins, John Clifford, John Taras, Richard Tanner, Todd Bolender, and Lorca Massine.

1972

New York City Ballet tours, to Munich for the Olympic Games, and to the Soviet Union.

1973

Publication of *The New York City Ballet* to celebrate the twenty-fifth anniversary of the company, with photographs by George Platt Lynes, who recorded the company and its predecessors from 1935 through 1955, and by Martha Swope.

1973

Presented the Handel Medallion by New York City.

1974

Publication of *Elie Nadelman*. Initiates the exhibition *The Sculpture and Drawings of Elie Nadelman*, shown at the Whitney and Hirshhorn Museums in 1975–1976.

1975

Publication of *Nijinsky Dancing*.

1975 MAY 14–31

The Ravel Festival of the New York City Ballet: New York State Theater. The opening attended by Madame Valéry Giscard-d'Estaing, representing the Government of France.

1976 MAY

The New York City Ballet produces *Union Jack*, choreographed by George Balanchine, as its contribution to the United States Bicentennial. Sir Peter Ramsbotham, Ambassador from the Court of St. James's, and the Earl of Harewood are guests at the opening.

1976

The Government of France invites the New York City Ballet to perform in Paris in honor of the United States Bicentennial.

1977

Publication of *Union Jack*.

PHOTOGRAPHS

Rochester, 1913

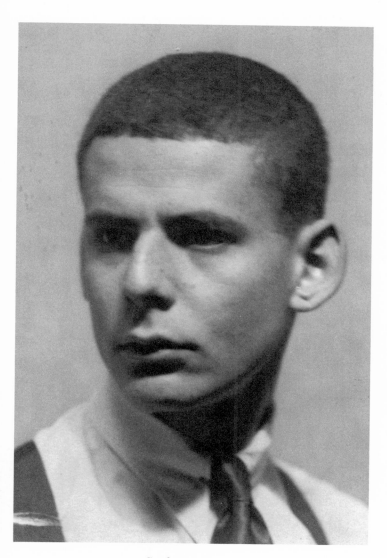

Cambridge, 1920s

Cambridge, 1931 Walker Evans

Hüngen, Bavaria, 1945

New York City, 1952 Cecil Beaton

Kyoto, 1969 Matusoki Nagare

Montgomery, Alabama, 1965 Harley Brate

New York City, 1960 Henri Cartier-Bresson

New York City, 1953 Feingersh-Pix

THE BIBLIOGRAPHY

*[Each section of the bibliography
is prefaced by an excerpt
from the author's writings.]*

FICTION

(From the novel *Flesh Is Heir* 1932)

Was it a guest they were expecting, thought Roger, or a ghost? All of his friends gathered to console themselves in their grief, would not Diaghilev come through the archway himself, and his gracious presence call them to a magic attention? Were they waiting him? And suddenly it seemed to Roger, as the car bore his eyes away from the house and from the picture of the quiet throng of dancers, as if a ballet was about to begin. The dancers were waiting for the conductor's rap on his music stand. They were all waiting, with their initial positions and attitudes soberly assumed, waiting for the curtain to go up.

And then Roger realized, and the realization clouded his eyes, that they were waiting only an end; this gathering was the end, the last noble congress that was to set a period at the end of an epoch. A dynasty had ended, the king was interred on the Island of Saint Michael among the marble headstones and the cypresses. The court in mourning met for a final few words before their ultimate and immediate dispersal. It was the end indeed, the end of youth for a distinguished company of human beings, the end of power and endeavor, the end perhaps of the first quarter of the twentieth century. . . . And yet how nobly, with what precise dignity, what consciousness of each separate personal role had these dancers performed the commencement, or the denouement of the last ballet. . . .

Roger and Christine sat in the boat that took them across the bay to Venice. It was growing dark, and high flying, ascending steel grey clouds hung above the city. . . . He turned up to the clouds again, and the feeling of anticipation, of immanence, definitely gave way to the feeling of finality. Roger considered how the clouds resolved themselves into an architecture of shifting mists. The mists became pillars and rough hewn blocks and balls. The pillars, blocks and balls dissolved into what but dancers. The sky was on the verge of another ballet. The clouds had become ballerinas. The sun before it set would set the action spinning, before they danced themselves into the dark. And as if waiting only for the first stroke of the orchestra, the last ray of sunlight lifted up the pink brightness of the approaching campanile, an unearthly baton raised to the sky. The shaft flashed for a moment in the sunlight. The conductor had commenced the overture, and Roger, shutting his eyes, dimmed the footlights.

So, he thought, however final, it is a continuation. The dancers feel that they must keep together. They will go on. They had to see each other at once whether or not Diaghilev died. That was a continuation, my being there, my happening in, was a continuation. Dissolve or not the forms must remain to be developed again. But he did not convince himself. His arguments were impelled too much by a desire for them to be so, he knew. He had seen in the faces of the dancers the inevitable recognition of finality.

(*Excerpt from numbers 1 and 3*)

BOOKS

1

Flesh Is Heir: An Historical Romance. New York: Brewer, Warren & Putnam, 1932. 311 pages.

    a. Carbondale and Edwardsville, Illinois: Southern Illinois University Press; London and Amsterdam: Feffer & Simons, 1975. 323 pages.

    b. New York: Popular Library, 1977. 255 pages.

2

For My Brother: A True Story by José Martínez Berlanga as Told to Lincoln Kirstein. London: The Hogarth Press, 1943. 189 pages.

    a. [Also issued by Macmillan Company of Canada, Toronto, 1943.]

3

From Flesh Is Heir: Two Unpublished Paragraphs. Lunenburg, [Vermont: Stinehour Press]; Verona: [Stamperia Valdonega]; Newport: [Fisher Press]; New York: [Spiral Press and Eakins Press Foundation], 1976. [9] pages. Illustrated. Half title: *For Lincoln, May the Fourth, 1976.* Edition of seventeen copies.

IN PERIODICALS

4

"The Silver Fan" [dramatic sketch]. *Phillips Exeter Monthly* 26:5 (Feb. 1922), 115–119.

5

"*De Fine Mundi.*" *The Dome* [Berkshire School, Sheffield, Massachusetts] 17:2 (Feb. 1923), 18–20. With an illustration by the author.

6

"Happy, Happy, Happy Pair." *The Dome* 17:4 (June 1923), 9–12.

7

"The Complete Whifflepink: Giovanni Strohmbi, 1729–1789(?)" [parody program note]. *Harvard Advocate* 113:5 (Jan. 1927), 21–26.

8

"Nothing at All: A Story." *Harper's Magazine* 165:4 (Sept. 1932), 436–443.

POETRY

(From *Rhymes of a PFC* 1964)

VAUDEVILLE

Pete Petersen, before this bit, a professional
    entertainer;
He and a partner tossed two girls on the Two-a-Day,
Swung them by their heels and snatched them in
    mid-air,
Billed as "Pete's Meteors: Acrobatic Adagio &
    Classical Ballet."

His vulnerable grin, efficiency, or bland physique
Lands him in Graves' Registration, a slot few strive
    to seek.
He follows death around picking up pieces,
Recovering men and portions of men so that by dawn
Only the landscape bares its wounds, the dead are gone.

Near Echternach, after the last stand they had the
    heart to make
With much personal slaughter by small arms at
    close range,
I drive for an officer sent down to look things over.
There is Pete slouched on a stump, catching his wind.

On your feet: salute. "Yes, sir?"
"Bad here, what?" "Yes, sir."

Good manners or knowing no word can ever condone
What happened, what he had to do, has done,

[47]

Spares further grief. Pete sits down.
A shimmering pulsation of exhaustion fixes him
In its throbbing aura like footlights when the curtain rises.
His act is over. Nothing now till the next show.

He takes his break while stagehands move the scenery,
And the performing dogs are led up from below.

PEACE

This was the end of a war:
   Here we were, rounding the bend,
Racing towards peace against time,
   Wild to be in at the end.
The front swept ahead like a flood
   Rolling away from our road;
We chased after the fading guns
   With hope our heaviest load.

For years we'd been one and one—
   Millions of ones, all apart;
The end of this war which everyone won
   Was time to unbuckle the heart.

Only a small border town;
   Bright banners hung to the ground;
Weather sighed thanks, everyone laughed,
   Brooks made a bubbly sound.
They said: "Take any bed here.
   Bathe in the brook by the gate.
Sleep through the steep or fading star.
   Don't wake up till it's late."

Poetry

I walked into a white room
   And found me a big double bed.
On its fresh crisp counterpane
   Glowed a curly gilt double head.

Its four lips made one mouth:
   His firm tawny arm lay free
Across the pulse of her childish breast.
   They were not startled by me.
I sat on the edge of their bed,
   Held his open hand in my hold;
Our fingers joined beneath the weight
   Of her fair hair's curly gold.

Linen sheets fold back from flesh;
   Tan skin is kissed by white.
Here's where we've all come to play
   Tonight and every night.

(*Poems from number 12*)

BOOKS AND PAMPHLETS

9

A Marriage Message for Mary Frost & James Maybon from Lincoln Kirstein: Paris, May 15, 1929. [Boston: the author], 1929. [6] pages. Edition of three copies.

10

Notre Dame des Cadres. New York: Modern Editions Press, [1933?]. [4] pages. (The Poetry Series, Pamphlet 1)

11

Low Ceiling. New York: G. P. Putnam's Sons, 1935. viii, 99 pages.

12

Rhymes of a PFC. New York: New Directions; Tokyo: John Weatherhill, 1964. vii, 179 pages.
    a. [Also issued by McClelland & Stewart, Toronto, 1964.]

13

Rhymes and More Rhymes of a PFC. New York: New Directions, 1966. viii, 215 pages.
Contents as *Rhymes of a PFC*, with some section titles changed and twenty additional poems.

IN BOOKS AND PERIODICALS

14

"A Garden Party in Simla." *The Dome* [Berkshire School, Sheffield, Massachusetts] 17:2 (Feb. 1923), 22. With an illustration by the author.

15

"Maudlin Meditations." *The Dome* 17:4 (June 1923), 33.

16

"March from the Ruins of Athens." *Harvard Advocate* 113:3 (Dec. 1926), 24–25.

17

"Between the Bells." *Hound & Horn* 1:1 (Sept. 1927), 26–27.
Included (retitled "Back to School") in *Low Ceiling* (11).

18

"Return Ticket Paid" [Parts I–III]. *Hound & Horn* 1:2
(Dec. 1927), 103–106.
Part III (revised and titled "Inventory") included in *Low
Ceiling* (11).

19

"Georgic." *Hound & Horn* 2:1 (Sept. 1928), 39–40.
Included in *Ten Introductions: A Collection of Modern Verse*
(21) and in *Low Ceiling* (11).

20

"Baby Gangster." *New English Weekly* 2:14 (Jan. 19, 1933),
333.
Included in *Low Ceiling* (11).

21

"Chamber of Horrors"; "Georgic"; "The Life of Byrne."
Pages 33–52 in *Ten Introductions: A Collection of Modern
Verse*, edited by Genevieve Taggard and Dudley Fitts. New
York: Arrow Editions, 1934.
Included in *Low Ceiling* (11).

22

"Memorial Window: 1946–56." *Nation* 182:22 (June 2,
1956), 467.
Included (retitled "Memorial") in *Rhymes of a PFC* (12).

23

"Das Schloss"; "Festspielhaus." *Massachusetts Review* 3:2
(Winter 1962), 269–274.
Included in *Rhymes of a PFC* (12).

24

"Threesome"; "K.P."; "Hijack"; "Black Joe"; "Vaudeville."
Hudson Review 15:4 (Winter 1962/63), 504–511.

"Vaudeville" is included in *The Norton Anthology of Modern Poetry* (31) and *Modern Poems: An Introduction to Poetry* (32); the five poems are included in *Rhymes of a PFC* (12).

25
"Tudoresque"; "Fixer." *Hudson Review* 17:1 (Spring 1964), 44–53.
Included in *Rhymes of a PFC* (12).

26
"U.N." *Hudson Review* 17:3 (Autumn 1964), 367–370.

27
"Eisenstein." *Massachusetts Review* 6:1 (Autumn/Winter 1964/65), 145–150.

28
"Western"; "Bar & Grill"; "Dead on Arrival." *Hudson Review* 19:3 (Autumn 1966), 391–397.

29
"March." *Massachusetts Review* 8:2 (Spring 1967), 247–250.

30
"Siegfriedslage." *Shenandoah* 18:2 (Winter 1967), 51–55.
  a. Reprinted, pages 50–55, in *For W. H. Auden, February 21, 1972*, edited by Peter H. Salus and Paul B. Taylor. New York: Random House, 1972.
  b. Reprinted, pages 128–130 (with "Postscript: Wystan at War," pages 130–133), in *W. H. Auden: A Tribute*, edited by Stephen Spender. New York: Macmillan, 1975.
  [Also issued by George Weidenfeld and Nicolson, London, 1975.]

31
"Fall In"; "Foresight"; "Vaudeville"; "Das Schloss"; "Bath." Pages 747–751 in *The Norton Anthology of Modern Poetry*, edited by Richard Ellmann and Robert O'Clair. New York: W. W. Norton, 1973.

"Fall In," "Vaudeville" and "Das Schloss" are included in *Rhymes of a PFC* (12). "Foresight" and "Bath" are included in *Rhymes and More Rhymes of a PFC* (13).

32
"Fall In"; "Vaudeville." Pages 288–290 in *Modern Poems: An Introduction to Poetry*, edited by Richard Ellmann and Robert O'Clair. New York: W. W. Norton, 1976.
Included in *Rhymes of a PFC* (12).

DRAMA AND BALLET
LIBRETTI

(Libretto for the ballet *Pocahontas* 1936)

When the English adventurers sailed into the bay form-
ed by the outlet of the Virginia rivers, they still thought
that the strange new land might be a part of the East
Indian Spice Isles. The people they found, subject to
King Powhatan, were by no means the red nomads of
our Western plains, but rather the gold-brown village-
dwelling hunters and farmers which have since completely disappeared.

When John Smith came here he was middle aged. He
had fought the Turks and was an experienced adventur-
er. He accepted the cruel tortures of Powhatan's braves
as the possible price of another adventure. But the ca-
pricious pity of a young Indian princess was something
new. Pocahontas seemed disgusted by the savagery of
her kinsmen. Instinctively she felt the dawn of a new
civilization. Yet the most acceptable gifts of the white
men were firearms and fire-water, scarcely an improve-
ment over tobacco and tomahawk. Guns and whiskey
purchased the Indians. A handful of English seized
America. Pocahontas married Rolfe, a young protégé of
Smith, was presented at the court of James I, and died in
England, bearing Rolfe's child. For us she symbolizes
the naive trust and inherent tragedy of original Ameri-
cans.

The general character and atmosphere of the ballet
were suggested by Hart Crane's "The Dance," a section of his longer poem "The Bridge."

1. Smith and Rolfe lost in the Virginia Forest

2. The Indians ambush John Smith

3. Princess Pocahontas and her Ladies

4. Smith is tortured by Indians and saved by Pocahontas

5. Smith presents young Rolfe to Pocahontas
   a.) Rolfe and Pocahontas dance

6. Pavane, Farewell of Indians, Pocahontas and Rolfe sail for England

(*Libretto for number 38*)

FULL-LENGTH PLAYS

33

White House Happening: A Didactic Collage, in a Prologue, Two Acts; an Epilogue. [Cambridge, Massachusetts], 1966. 172 pages. Reproduced from typescript; prepared for performances at the Loeb Drama Center, Harvard University, August 1967.

34

Magic Carpet: A Farce or Fable in Two Acts. [Cambridge, Massachusetts], 1967. 154 pages. Reproduced from typescript; prepared for a reading at the Harvard Dramatic Club, January 18, 1968.

BALLET LIBRETTI

In the listing of libretti, performance has been considered publication; the texts have not appeared separately in print with the exception of *The Spellbound Child.*

35

Transcendence. Choreography: George Balanchine. Music: Franz Liszt (orchestration by George Antheil). Decor: Gaston Longchamp. Costumes: Franklin Watkins. First performance: Avery Memorial Theater, Hartford, Connecticut, December 6, 1934; Producing Company of the School of American Ballet. Premiere: Adelphi Theater, New York, March 5, 1935; the American Ballet.

36

The Bat. Choreography: George Balanchine. Music: Johann Strauss. Costumes: Keith Martin. Premiere: Metropolitan Opera House, New York, May 20, 1936; the American Ballet.

37

Harlequin for President. Choreography: Eugene Loring. Music: Domenico Scarlatti. Costumes: Keith Martin. Premiere: Bennington College, July 17, 1936; Ballet Caravan.

38

Pocahontas. Choreography: Lew Christensen. Music: Elliott Carter, Jr. Costumes: Karl Free. Premiere: Bennington College, July 18, 1936; Ballet Caravan.

39

Yankee Clipper. Choreography: Eugene Loring. Music: Paul Bowles. Costumes: Charles Rain. Premiere: Town Hall, Saybrook, Connecticut, July 12, 1937; Ballet Caravan.

40

Filling Station. Choreography: Lew Christensen. Music: Virgil Thomson. Decor and costumes: Paul Cadmus. Premiere: Avery Memorial Theater, Hartford, Connecticut, January 6, 1938; Ballet Caravan.

41

Billy the Kid. Choreography: Eugene Loring. Music: Aaron Copland. Decor and costumes: Jared French. Premiere: Chicago Civic Theater, October 16, 1938; Ballet Caravan.

42

Charade (or, The Debutante). Choreography: Lew Christensen. Music: American melodies, arranged by Trude Rittman. Decor and costumes: Alvin Colt. Premiere: Lancaster, Pennsylvania, October 17, 1939; Ballet Caravan.

43

City Portrait. Choreography: Eugene Loring. Music: Henry Brant. Costumes: Forrest Thayr, Jr. Premiere: Four Arts Club, Mobile, Alabama, October 23, 1939; Ballet Caravan.

44

Juke Box. Choreography: William Dollar. Music: Alec Wilder. Decor and costumes: Tom Lee. First performance: Little Theatre of Hunter College, New York, May 27, 1941; American Ballet Caravan. Premiere: Teatro Municipal, Rio de Janeiro, July 4, 1941; American Ballet Caravan.

Drama and Ballet Libretti

45
Time Table. Choreography: Antony Tudor. Music: Aaron Copland. Decor and costumes: James Stewart Morcom. Premiere: Hunter College Playhouse, New York, May 29, 1941; American Ballet Caravan.

46
The Spellbound Child (*L'Enfant et les Sortilèges*), poem by Colette, translated by Lincoln Kirstein and Jane Barzin. Choreography: George Balanchine. Music: Maurice Ravel. Decor and costumes: Aline Bernstein. Premiere: Central High School of Needle Trades, New York, November 20, 1946; Ballet Society. (*See item 187*)

47
The Minotaur, with Joan Junyer. Choreography: John Taras. Music: Elliott Carter, Jr. Decor and costumes: Joan Junyer. Premiere: Central High School of Needle Trades, New York, March 26, 1947; Ballet Society.

ON DANCE

(From *Dance Index: George Balanchine* 1945)

George Balanchine, to anyone upon whom dancing exercises its enchantment, must always seem the sorcerer, different in scope and scale from other contemporary choreographers. His best works are all classical, and though he can compose for the individual dancer better than anyone else in the Western world, his ballets are created apart from the dancers who appear in them and they can be given a new interpretation by any notable talent fortunate enough to perform them. . . . These classical ballets will serve as the base for future repertories much as the works of Petipa and Ivanov have served in the past. The next generation will use Balanchine's work as a standard for style and asymmetrical extension, the grand contemporary academy of the development of the capabilities of the human body on the largest possible scale. . . . When he reads a score all the musical elements, the components of counterpoint, harmony, rhythm and melody, are richly suggested to him, not as a series of Tableaux Vivants, but as sequence of spatial and mobile notions of anatomical relationships, less literary than melodic. An entrance, —a fanfare of movement, —a single exit, —a sweep emptying the stage, come forth as abstract compositional patterns used to support the music, or emphasize its break, silence, or recommencement, or for their own sake, or as part of the mysterious, hidden 'floor' of dancing, which is his orchestral score. His dance achieves a magic of its own; the exterior world is in comparison Shakespeare's unsubstantial world of images; and every apparently meaningless gesture has its proper significance, if not on the obvious level of logic, then on the profounder level of physical necessity or instinct.

(*Excerpt from number 151*)

(From *The Classic Ballet* 1952)

The most powerful theatrical essence remains, where it began, in the dance. Its capacity to astonish by brilliance or calm by harmony provides a physical frame in which artist-craftsmen may demonstrate the happier chances of the race, symbolized by the dancer's determined conquest of habitual physical limitation. . . . The classic style, supported by its academic technique, depends upon rigid criteria and severe discipline for even a modest executant efficiency, like our music, medicine, and architecture, but unlike our prose, poetry or painting. . . . In liberal democracy and anxious anarchy, the traditional classic dance, compact of aristocratic authority and absolute freedom in a necessity of order, has never been so promising as an independent expression as it is today. At the moment, when representational art has declined into subjective expressionism, and its chief former subject, the human body in space, has been atomized into rhetorical calligraphy, the academic dance is a fortress of its familiar if forgotten dignity. To it future painters and sculptors may one day return for instruction in its wide plastic use.

(*Excerpt from number 65*)

BOOKS

48

Nijinsky [in anonymous collaboration with Romola Nijinsky].
London: Victor Gollancz, 1933. 416 pages. Illustrated.
  a. [Also issued by Ryerson Press, Toronto, 1933.]
  b. Paris: Denoël et Steele, [1934]. Translated by Pierre
     Dutray, with a preface by Paul Claudel. 425 pages.
  c. New York: Simon and Schuster, 1934. Foreword by
     Paul Claudel. xvii, 447 pages. Illustrated.
     [Also issued by Musson Book Company, Toronto,
     1934.]
  d. [Budapest: Nyugat kiadó és irodalmi, [1935?]. Trans-
     lated by Lydia Lengyel. 384 pages. Illustrated.]
  e. [New York: Garden City Publishing Company, 1941.
     Reprint of the 1934 Simon and Schuster edition.]
     [Also issued by Blue Ribbon Books, Toronto, 1941.]
  f. [New York: Grosset & Dunlap, 1960. 460 pages.]
     [Also issued by Mayflower Publishing Company, Lon-
     don, 1960.]
  g. [New York: Pocket Books, 1972. Foreword by Paul
     Claudel. 369 pages. Illustrated.]

49

Fokine. With an introduction by Arnold L. Haskell. London:
British-Continental Press, 1934. 67 pages. Illustrated. (The
Artists of the Dance, 12)
  a. Partially reprinted, pages 7–17, in *Carnaval, Le Spectre
     de la Rose and Les Sylphides*, by Lincoln Kirstein, Arnold
     L. Haskell and Stewart Deas. London: The Bodley
     Head, for the Governors of Sadler's Wells Foundations,
     1949. (Sadler's Wells Ballet Books, 4)
  b. [Reprinted by University Microfilms, Ann Arbor,
     Michigan.]

50

Dance: A Short History of Classic Theatrical Dancing. New
York: G. P. Putnam's Sons, 1935. ix, 369 pages. Illustrated.
  a. Reissued with additional material as *The Book of the*

Dance: A Short History of Classic Theatrical Dancing. Garden City, New York: Garden City Publishing Company, 1942. ix, 388 pages. Illustrated.
[Also issued by Blue Ribbon Books, Toronto, 1942.]

    b. Reissued with further additional material as *Dance: A Short History of Classic Theatrical Dancing.* Brooklyn: Dance Horizons, 1969. xi, 398 pages. Illustrated.

    c. [*Dance: A Short History of Classic Theatrical Dancing.* Westport, Connecticut: Greenwood Press, 1970. Reprint of the 1935 Putnam's edition.]

51

Blast at Ballet: A Corrective for the American Audience. New York: [the author], 1938. 128 pages.

    a. Reprinted in *Three Pamphlets Collected* (55).

    b. [Reprinted by University Microfilms, Ann Arbor, Michigan.]

52

Ballet Alphabet: A Primer for Laymen. With drawings by Paul Cadmus. New York: Kamin Publishers, 1939. 71 pages.

    a. Reprinted in *Three Pamphlets Collected* (55).

53

What Ballet Is about: An American Glossary. With a portfolio of photographs of the New York City Ballet by Martha Swope. Brooklyn: Dance Perspectives, 1959. 80 pages. (Dance Perspectives, 1)

    a. Reprinted (without photographs) in *Three Pamphlets Collected* (55).

    b. [Reprinted by Johnson Reprint Corporation, New York, 1970.]

54

Gagaku: The Music and Dances of the Japanese Imperial Household. Edited and with an introduction by Lincoln Kirstein. Text by Robert Garfias; calligraphy by Yasuhide Kobashi. New York: Theatre Arts Books, 1959. [40] pages. Illustrated.

55

Three Pamphlets Collected: Blast at Ballet, 1937 [i.e. 1938]; *Ballet Alphabet, 1939; What Ballet Is All about* [sic], *1959.* With a new foreword. Brooklyn: Dance Horizons, 1967. Original paginations retained. (Dance Horizons Republication, 9)

56

Movement & Metaphor: Four Centuries of Ballet. New York and Washington: Praeger Publishers, 1970. viii, 290 pages. Illustrated.

    a. [Also issued by Pitman, London, 1971.]

57

The New York City Ballet. With photographs by Martha Swope and George Platt Lynes. New York: Alfred A. Knopf, 1973. 261 pages.

    a. [Also issued by A. & C. Black, London, 1974.]

58

For John Martin: Entries from an Early Diary [June–August, 1933]. New York: Dance Perspectives Foundation, 1973. 56 pages. Illustrated. (Dance Perspectives, 54)

59

Nijinsky Dancing. With photographs by Bert, de Meyer, Druet, Roosen, White, and others; and essays by Jacques Rivière and Edwin Denby. New York: Alfred A. Knopf, 1975. 177 pages.

    a. [Also issued by Thames and Hudson, London, 1975.]

60

Union Jack. Edited and with texts by Lincoln Kirstein; photographs by Martha Swope and Richard Benson. New York: Eakins Press Foundation, 1977. 107 pages.

IN BOOKS

61

"Kirstein 1937" [on Martha Graham]. Pages 23–33 in *Martha Graham*, edited by Merle Armitage. Los Angeles: [the editor], 1937.

62

"Ballet and Music." Pages 108–118 in *The International Cyclopedia of Music and Musicians*, edited by Oscar Thompson. New York: Dodd, Mead, 1939 and subsequent editions.
>   a. Reprinted, pages 298–317, in *The Music Lover's Handbook*, edited by Elie Siegmeister. New York: William Morrow, 1943.

63

"Achievement." Page 9 in [*The Year Book of*] *The Ballet Society: 1946–1947*. New York: Ballet Society, 1947.

64

"Foreword." Pages ix–x in *The Dance Encyclopedia*, compiled and edited by Anatole Chujoy. New York: A. S. Barnes, 1949.

65

"The Classic Ballet: Historical Development." Pages 3–17 in *The Classic Ballet: Basic Technique and Terminology*, by Muriel Stuart. New York: Alfred A. Knopf, 1952.
>   a. [Also issued by McClelland & Stewart, Toronto, 1952.]
>   b. Also issued by Longmans, Green, London, 1953. [Reissued by A. & C. Black, London, 1977.]
>   c. Pages 1–18 in *Kurashikku Baree* (Japanese translation by R. Matsumoto and K. Mori). Tokyo: Ongaku no Yusha, 1967.

66

"Alec: or, the Future of Choreography." Pages 41–53 in *Dance News Annual* [*1*]: *1953*, edited by Winthrop Palmer and Anatole Chujoy. New York: Alfred A. Knopf, 1953.

67

"The Ballet in Hartford." Pages 63–74 in *A. Everett Austin, Jr.: A Director's Taste and Achievement*. Hartford, Connecticut: Wadsworth Atheneum, 1958.

68

"Introduction." Pages vii–viii in *The Dance Encyclopedia*, revised and enlarged edition, compiled and edited by Anatole Chujoy and P. W. Manchester. New York: Simon and Schuster, 1967.

69

"The New York City Ballet." Pages 6–18 in *Ballet & Modern Dance*. London: Octopus Books, 1974. Illustrated.

70

"Delibes and *Coppélia*." Pages 26–29 in *Coppélia*, text by Nancy Goldner and Lincoln Kirstein; photographs by Richard Benson. New York: Eakins Press Foundation, 1974.

71

"Introduction." Pages 5–9 in *The Nutcracker: The Story of the New York City Ballet's Production Told in Pictures by Martha Swope*, edited by Nancy Lassalle. New York: Dodd, Mead, 1975.
  a. Partially reprinted, pages [3–4, 12], in *Playbill* (New York State Theater issue, Dec. 4, 1975–Jan. 4, 1976) [program]. New York: American Theatre Press, 1975–1976. Illustrated.

72

"Introduction." Pages 5–7 in *A Midsummer Night's Dream: The Story of the New York City Ballet's Production Told in Photographs by Martha Swope*, edited by Nancy Lassalle. New York: Dodd, Mead, 1977.

73

"Rationale of a Repertory." Pages 1–12 in *Repertory in Review: 40 Years of the New York City Ballet*, by Nancy Reynolds. New York: Dial Press, 1977.

ARTICLES AND REVIEWS

74

"The Diaghilev Period." *Hound & Horn* 3:4 (July/Sept. 1930), 468–501. Illustrated.

75

"Dance Chronicle: Kreutzberg; Wigman; *Pas d'Acier* [Strawbridge-Prokofiev-Simonson]; The Future." *Hound & Horn* 4:4 (July/Sept. 1931), 573–580.

76

"Homage to Michel Fokine." *New English Weekly* 3:15 (July 27, 1933), 350–351.

77

"'Modern Dance' and Dancing" [Isadora Duncan, Mary Wigman, Anna Pavlova, and others]. *New English Weekly* 3:18 (Aug. 17, 1933), 421.

78

"Ballet" [Diaghilev, Lifar, Boris Kochno, Kurt Jooss, Balanchine, Les Ballets 1933, Ballet Russe de Monte Carlo, Original Ballet Russe, and others]. *Vogue* 82:9 (Nov. 1, 1933), 28–31, 102–103. Illustrated.

79

"The School of the American Ballet." *Hound & Horn* 7:2 (Jan./March 1934), 284–286.

80

"The Dance: The Persistence of Ballet" [Vachtang Chabukiani, Vecheslova, Monte Carlo Ballet Russe; Balanchine, and the School of American Ballet]. *Nation* 138 (No. 3578, Jan. 31, 1934), 138–140.

81

"The Dance: The Music Hall; Revues; the Movies" [Florence Rogge and the Roxyettes, Barry and Coe, Buck and Bubbles, the Ziegfeld Follies and Patricia Bowman, Vilma and Buddy

Ebsen, Snake Hips, Bill Robinson, Fred Astaire, Charles
Weidman, Busby Berkeley]. *Nation* 138 (No. 3584, March
14, 1934), 310–311.

82

"Nijinsky" [review of] *Nijinsky*, by Romola Nijinsky [in
anonymous collaboration with Lincoln Kirstein]. *Nation* 138
(No. 3588, April 11, 1934), 420.

83

"Prejudice Purely" [on Martha Graham]. *New Republic* 78
(No. 1010, April 11, 1934), 243–244.

84

"Correspondence" [letter on classical ballet and modern
dance]. *Dance Observer* 1:4 (May 1934), 47–48.

85

"In Defense of the Ballet." *Modern Music* 11:4 (May/June
1934), 189–194.

86

"The Dance: 'Cotillion' [Balanchine-Chabrier-Bérard]; 'Union
Pacific' [Massine-Nabokov-MacLeish]" [Monte Carlo Ballet Russe]. *Nation* 138 (No. 3592, May 9, 1934), 546.

87

"The Dance: 'Kykunkor'; Native African Opera." *Nation* 138
(No. 3597, June 13, 1934), 684.

88

"Revolutionary Ballet Forms" [Fokine, Nijinsky, Massine,
Bronislava Nijinska, Balanchine, the School of American
Ballet]. *New Theatre* 1:9 (Oct. 1934), 12–14. Illustrated.

89

"The Dance: Some American Dancers" [Martha Graham,
Mary Wigman, Helen Tamiris, Doris Humphries and Charles
Weidman, Agnes de Mille, Roger Pryor Dodge, and others].
Nation 140 (No. 3634, Feb. 27, 1935), 258–259.

90

"The Dance as Theatre" [classical ballet opposed to modern dance]. *New Theatre* 2:5 (May 1935), 20–22.

91

"Is Ballet Alive?" *Theatre Arts Monthly* 19:8 (Aug. 1935), 639–640.

92

"The Dance: A Letter" [on John Martin's attitude toward ballet, the School of American Ballet, and the American Ballet company]. New York *Times* (Aug. 25, 1935), section 10, page 5.

93

"The Ballet Is Classic" [responding to "Make the Dance American," by Ruth St. Denis]. *Current Controversy* 1:2 (Nov. 1935), 17, 39.

94

"Scenery for Theatrical Dancing" [Bakst, Benois, Larionov, Goncharova, Picasso and the School of Paris, the Constructivists, Miró, Tchelitchew, Noguchi, Calder, and others]. *Art Front* 2:2 (Jan. 1936), 12–13. Illustrated.

95

"Progress of M. Balanchine in Choreographic Field Cited by Kirstein" [letter]. New York *Evening Journal,* Final Night Extra edition (Feb. 28, 1936), 24.

96

"Away from the Home of the Ballet" [review of] *Russian Somersault,* by Igor Schwezoff. *New York Herald Tribune Books* (March 8, 1936), 6. Illustrated.

97

"A Museum of Ballet" [Monte Carlo Ballet Russe]. *New Theatre* 3:6 (June 1936), 20–21, 37. Illustrated.

98

"Ballet and the Modern Dance Today." *Dance* 1:1 (Oct. 1936), 6, 26. Illustrated.

99

"The Stepchild of the Arts" [review of] *American Dancing: The Background and Personalities of the Modern Dance*, by John Martin. *New York Herald Tribune Books* (Dec. 13, 1936), 31.

100

"Crisis in the Dance" [on classical ballet and modern dance]. *North American Review* 243:1 (Spring 1937), 80–103.

101

"Working with Stravinsky" [*Jeu de Cartes* (*The Card Party: Ballet in Three Deals*)]. *Modern Music* 14:3 (March/April 1937), 143–146.
   a. Reprinted, pages 136–140, in *Stravinsky in the Theatre*, edited by Minna Lederman. New York: Pellegrini & Cudahy, 1949. Illustrated.

102

"Homage to Stravinsky." *Arts and Decoration* 46:3 (May 1937), 14–15, 46. Illustrated.

103

"An American Institution Is Founded" [School of American Ballet]. *Dance* 2:3; 4 (June; July 1937), 15–16, 37; 12–13.
   a. Reprinted, pages 27–33, in *School of American Ballet* [prospectus, 1937?].

104

"Ballet: Introduction and Credo." *Dance Observer* 4:8 (Oct. 1937), 94.

105

"The Ballet: Sad but Hopeful" [Massine, Catherine Little-field, the Jooss Ballet]. *Dance Observer* 4:9 (Nov. 1937), 113.

106

"Dance: The Monte Carlo Season" [Original Ballet Russe]. *Nation* 145:20 (Nov. 13, 1937), 541–542.

107

"The Ballet: Tyranny and Blackmail" [on dance criticism]. *Dance Observer* 4:10 (Dec. 1937), 129.

108

"To Dance" [exhibitions and performances at Rockefeller Center, "Dance International 1900–1937"]. *Town & Country* 92 (No. 4183, Dec. 1937), 128, 178.

109

"Dance International 1900–1937" [exhibitions and performances at Rockefeller Center]. *Dance Observer* 5:1 (Jan. 1938), 6–7.

110

"Dance through the Ages" [review of] *World History of the Dance*, by Curt Sachs, translated by Bessie Schoenberg. *Nation* 146:3 (Jan. 15, 1938), 74, 76.

111

"Dance: The Critic's Lexicon" [John Martin]. *Nation* 146:6 (Feb. 5, 1938), 164–166.

112

"Popular Style in American Dancing" [Fred Astaire, Hal Le Roy, Eleanor Powell, Ginger Rogers, Paul Draper, Vernon Castle, Buddy Ebsen, Buster West, Ray Bolger, and others]. *Nation* 146:16 (April 16, 1938), 450–451.

113

"Dance Documentary" [review of] *Complete Book of Ballets*, by Cyril W. Beaumont. *Nation* 146:22 (May 28, 1938), 622–623.

114

"Stardom: Slav and Native." *Dance* 4:3 (June 1938), 14–15. Illustrated.

115

"Our Ballet and Our Audience: The Ballet Caravan Tours to Havana." *American Dancer* 11:9 (July 1938), 22–23. Illustrated.

116

"Martha Graham at Bennington." *Nation* 147:10 (Sept. 3, 1938), 230–231.

117

"About 'Billy the Kid' " [Loring-Copland]. *Dance Observer* 5:8 (Oct. 1938), 116.

118

"Ballet 'Round the World" [review of] *Dancing Around the World*, by Arnold L. Haskell. Boston *Evening Transcript* (Nov. 5, 1938), section 4, page 2.

119

"Transcontinental Caravan" Parts 1 and 2 [Ballet Caravan American tour]. *Dance* 5:5; 6 (Feb.; March 1939), 14–15; 8, 38. Illustrated.

120

"About Dancers" [review of] *Artists of the Dance*, by Lillian Moore. *Kenyon Review* 1:2 (Spring 1939), 222–223.

121

"The Dance of Forever" [on the future of classic dance]. *Dance* 6:1 (April 1939), 11.

122

"Good Dance Book" [review of] *Dances of Our Pioneers*, by Grace L. Ryan. Boston *Evening Transcript* (July 15, 1939), section 4, page 1.

123

"American Saturday Night" [the square dance]. *Harper's Bazaar* 73:9 (Aug. 1939), 64–65, 108. Illustrated.

124

"Pas de Deux in 2 x 4" [televising dance: a Ballet Caravan

pas de deux with Lew Christensen and Gisella Caccialanza; Martha Graham's *Lamentation*]. *TAC Magazine* 2:1 (Sept. 1939), 15.

125
"Audience." *Dance Observer* 6:9 (Nov. 1939), 282–283.

126
"In Memoriam: Serge de Diaghileff." *Dance* 6:6 (Nov. 1939), 8. Illustrated.

127
"Album of Dancers" [review of] *The Book of the Ballets*, edited by Gerald Goode. Boston *Evening Transcript* (Nov. 18, 1939), section 4, page 1.

128
"Decor and Costume: Boston Balletomanes Can Turn to Book as Some Consolation for a Poor Season" [review of] *Five Centuries of Ballet Design*, by Cyril W. Beaumont. Boston *Evening Transcript* (Jan. 20, 1940), section 6, page 1.

129
"Kirstein Blasts Open Shop" [letter on labor relations]. *Dance* 7:4 (March 1940), 8.

130
"To the Editors" [letter on labor relations]. *Dance Observer* 7:5 (May 1940), 74.

131
"Eccentric Dancing" [Buddy Ebsen, the Marx Brothers, Charlie Chaplin, Ray Bolger, Nijinsky, Massine, and others]. *Theatre Arts* 24:6 (June 1940), 443–449. Illustrated.

132
"Ballet: Record and Augury" [Monte Carlo Ballet Russe, Ballet Russe de Monte Carlo, Original Ballet Russe, American Ballet, Ballet Caravan, Ballet Theatre]. *Theatre Arts* 24:9 (Sept. 1940), 650–659. Illustrated.

133

"The Indians Dance" [ritual dances of the American Southwest]. *Harper's Bazaar* 74:10 (Sept. 1, 1940), 68–69, 98, 100–101. Illustrated.

134

"Ballet Blitz: This Season Promises a Three-for-all" [Ballet Russe de Monte Carlo, Original Ballet Russe, Ballet Theatre]. *Town & Country 95* (No. 4217, Oct. 1940), 64–65, 102, 106. Illustrated.

135

"Dance in Review: Ballet Russe de Monte Carlo." *Dance* 8:4 (Nov. 1940), 5, 18.

136

"Drawings of Dancers." *Theatre Arts* 24:11 (Nov. 1940), 809–814. Illustrated.

137

"Lifar on Diaghilev" [review of] *Serge Diaghilev: His Life, His Work, His Legend*, by Serge Lifar. *Nation* 151:20 (Nov. 16, 1940), 481–483.

138

"Dear Editor" [letter on the Original Ballet Russe *Paganini* (Fokine-Rachmaninov)]. *PM's Weekly* 1:24 (Dec. 1, 1940), 47.

139

"Foreword" to "The Dance Archives." *Museum of Modern Art Bulletin* 8:3 (Feb./March 1941), 2.

140

"This Month in the Dance: Russian Ballet; Direction by Default" [Ballet Russe de Monte Carlo, Original Ballet Russe]. *Decision* 1:3 (March 1941), 81–83.

141

"This Month in the Dance: Home Team; The Ballet Theatre." *Decision* 1:4 (April 1941), 77–79.

142

"The American Ballet in Brazil: Part I of a Travel Diary." *American Dancer* 14:11 (Sept. 1941), 8–9, 19, 23. Illustrated.

143

"The American Ballet in Argentina: Part II of a Travel Diary." *American Dancer* 14:12 (Oct. 1941), 12–13, 25, 29. Illustrated.

144

"The American Ballet in Chile: Part III of a Travel Diary." *American Dancer* 15:1 (Nov. 1941), 10–11, 31. Illustrated.

145

"The American Ballet on the West Coast [Peru, Colombia, Venezuela]: Part IV of a Travel Diary." *American Dancer* 15:2 (Dec. 1941), 16–17, 30. Illustrated.

146

"Isadora Duncan." *Museum of Modern Art Bulletin* 9:2 (Nov. 1941), 10–11. Illustrated.

147

"Latin American Music for Ballet" [Paul Bowles, Francisco Mignone, Camargo Guarnieri, Alberto Ginastera, Domingo Santa Cruz, and others]. *Theatre Arts* 26:5 (May 1942), 329–335. Illustrated.

148

"Comment" [introduction to the issue *An Album of Nijinsky Photographs* with text by Edwin Denby]. *Dance Index* 2:3 (March 1943), 23.

149

"Comment" [introduction to the issue *The Romantic Ballet in London* with text by George Chaffee]. *Dance Index* 2:9/12 (Sept./Dec. 1943), 119.

150

"Comment" [introduction to the issue *Anna Pavlova: Notes by Marianne Moore*]. *Dance Index* 3:3 (March 1944), 35.

151

"Comment" [introduction to the issue *George Balanchine* with texts by Balanchine, Agnes de Mille, Edwin Denby]. *Dance Index* 4:2/3 (Feb./March 1945), 19.

152

"Comment" [introduction to the issue *The Criticism of Edwin Denby. Photographs by Walker Evans*]. *Dance Index* 5:2 (Feb. 1946), 27.

153

"Comment" [introduction to the issue *Isadora in Art* with text by Allan Ross Macdougall]. *Dance Index* 5:3 (March 1946), 59–60.

154

"Comment" [introduction to the issue *Dance Notation, by Juana de Laban*]. *Dance Index* 5:4/5 (April/May 1946), 87.

155

"Kyra Blanc: In Memoriam." *Dance News* 8:5 (May 1946), 4.

156

"Comment" [introduction to the issue *Clowns, Elephants and Ballerinas* arranged and with comments by Joseph Cornell]. *Dance Index* 5:6 (June 1946), 135.

157

"Comment" [introduction to the issue *Marius Petipa* with text by Yury Slonimsky]. *Dance Index* 6:5/6 (May/June 1947), 99.

158

"Balanchine Musagète" [*Apollon Musagète* and other collaborations with Stravinsky]. *Theatre Arts* 31:11 (Nov. 1947), 36–41. Illustrated.

    a. Reprinted (without illustrations), pages 202–209, in *Theatre Arts Anthology*, edited by Rosamond Gilder and others. New York: Theatre Arts Books, 1950.

159

"Balanchine and the Classic Revival." *Theatre Arts* 31:12 (Dec. 1947), 37–43. Illustrated.

160

"The Legacy of Diaghilew." *Dance News* 15:2 (Aug. 1949), 5, 6. Illustrated.

161

"Balanchine and American Ballet: With American Paintings of the Symbolic Realist School." Parts I and II. *Ballet* 9:5; 6 (May; June 1950), 24–33; 15–22. Illustrated.

162

"The Dance: Repertory; Ballet Director Suggests Some Formula Might Help in Creating Ballets." New York *Times* (July 9, 1950), section 2, page 2.

163

"Martin of *The Times*" [John Martin]. *Dance News* 20:4 (April 1952), 8.

164

"Repertory: The Face of the Company" [New York City Ballet]. *Center* 1:4 (June/July 1954), 20–23. Illustrated.

165

"The Monument of Diaghilev." *Dance News* 25:1 (Sept. 1954), 7. Illustrated.

166

"The Position of Balanchine: A New Design for Ballet." *Perspectives USA* 12 (Summer 1955), 77–82. Illustrated.
   a. Reprinted (without illustrations), pages 211–215, in *Salmagundi* 33/34 (Spring/Summer 1976).

167

"Arthur Bronson." *Dance News* 28:5 (May 1956), 9.

168

"To Do Again" [summary of the work with Balanchine since 1933]. *Theatre Arts* 42:9 (Sept. 1958), 68–70. Illustrated.

169

"The Nature of American Ballet: Balanchine, Robbins and the Creation of a Style." *Times Literary Supplement* Special Number, "The American Imagination" (Nov. 6, 1959), xxv. Illustrated.

    a. Reprinted, pages 97–103, in *The American Imagination: A Critical Survey of the Arts from the Times Literary Supplement.* London: Cassell, 1960.
    [Also issued by Atheneum, New York, 1960.]

170

"Ballet Has Own Logic: Music, Anatomy, Geometry Are Skilfully Combined." Spokane [Washington] *Spokesman-Review* (July 15, 1962), Family Section part 2, page 12.

171

"In Appreciation: John Martin." *Dance News* 41:1 (Sept. 1962), 3. Illustrated.

172

"Astonishing Reply" [letter on Nijinsky, Cocteau, Diaghilev]. *Nation* 196:7 (Feb. 16, 1963), facing 129.

173

"The Map of Movement" [review of] *The Choreographic Art: An Outline of Its Principles and Craft*, by Peggy Van Praagh and Peter Brinson. *Times Literary Supplement* 63 (No. 3229, Jan. 16, 1964), 37–38.

174

"Kirstein Argues about Petrouchka" [letter on Clive Barnes' review of the Joffrey Ballet revival of the Fokine-Stravinsky-Benois production]. New York *Times* (May 31, 1970), section 2, page 15.

175

"Balanchine's Fourth Dimension: His Eyes and Mind Transform Sound into Sight." *Vogue* 160:10 (Dec. 1972), 118–129, 203, 205–206. Illustrated.

176

"Balanchine Trio" [*Prodigal Son, The Four Temperaments, Agon*]. *About the House* 4:1 (Christmas 1972), 12–15. Illustrated.
    a. Reprinted (with variant illustrations), pages 186–187, in *Dancing Times* 63 (No. 748, Jan. 1973).

177

"Melissa Hayden: A Tribute." *Dance Magazine* 48:8 (Aug. 1973), 32–34. Illustrated.

178

"The Increased Popularity of Ballet in America." *Schwann-1 Record & Tape Guide* 26:5 (May 1974), 24–27. Illustrated.
    a. Reprinted (with variant illustrations), pages 10, 15, 17, 19, in *Playbill, New York State Theater Edition* 9 (Nov. 12–Dec. 1, 1974). New York: American Theatre Press, 1974.
    b. Reprinted (without illustrations, titled "Modern Ballet: A Moral Ordering"), pages 26–28, in *About the House* 4:12 (Summer 1976).

179

"Léo Delibes and the Inscape of *Coppélia*." *Dance and Dancers* 26:3 (March 1975), 28–29, 38. Illustrated.

PROGRAM AND OTHER NOTES

180

"The Ballet Caravan." Pages [1–2] in *Ballet Caravan* [prospectus, 1937?].

181

[Statement.] Page [4] in *The Ballet Caravan* [announcement, 1937/1938 season].

182

"Ballet Caravan." Pages [2–3] in *Ballet Caravan* [souvenir program, 1937/1938].

183

"The Ballet Caravan." In *The Ballet Caravan* [announcement, January 6 and 7, 1938 performances at the Avery Memorial Auditorium, Hartford, Connecticut]. 1 leaf.

184

"Report of the Director for the Year Ending June 30, 1941." Pages 5–6 in *The School of American Ballet* [catalogue, 1941/1942].

185

"Report of the Director for the Year Ending June 27, 1942." Pages 5–7 in *The School of American Ballet* [catalogue, Fall/Winter 1942/1943].

186

"1933–1944." Pages 4–7 in *School of American Ballet* [catalogue, 1944/1945].

187

"*The Spellbound Child*, Poem by Colette," translated by Lincoln Kirstein and Jane Barzin. Pages [7–12] in *The Ballet Society: First Program; November 20, 1946—Central High School of Needle Trades, 225 West 24th Street* [New York]. New York: Ballet Society, 1946.

    a. Reprinted in *Voices* 138 (Summer 1949), 8–17.
    b. Reprinted, pages [13–14], in *New York City Ballet: Hommage à Ravel, 1875–1975* [souvenir program for the performances May 14–31, 1975]. New York: Souvenir Book Publishers, 1975.

188

The Nutcracker [souvenir program, 1954], edited by Lincoln Kirstein. New York: Souvenir Programs, [1954]. [24] pages. Illustrated.

189

[Statement.] Pages [3–4] in "George Platt Lynes," text for *New York City Ballet: Photographs from 1935 through 1955 Taken by George Platt Lynes, 1907–1956* [souvenir program, 1957]. New York: Souvenir Programs, 1957.

190

"Our Dancers' Debt." Pages 11–13, 15 in *Playbill* (Metropolitan Opera House issue, April 16–May 9, 1959). New York: Playbill, 1959.

191

"1934–1959." Pages [4–6] in *School of American Ballet* [catalogue, 1959/1960].

192

"A Building as a Ballerina." Pages [3–9] in *The City Center of Music and Drama Presents the New York City Ballet at the New York State Theater, Lincoln Center* [souvenir program, 1964]. New York: Program Publishing Company, 1964. Illustrated.

193

[Introduction to] "Edwin Denby on the Dance." Pages 8–9 in *New York State Theater Magazine* 1:1, 2 (March 29–May 22, 1966) [program]. New York: Playbill, 1966.

194

"A Subscription Audience for Ballet." Pages 30–31 in *New York State Theater Magazine* 1:1 (March 29–May 6, 1966) [program]. New York: Playbill, 1966.

195

[Statement.] Pages [3–4] in *Morton Baum: Chairman of the Board of the City Center of Music and Drama, Inc.; December 28, 1905–February 7, 1968.* [New York: 1968.]

196

"An Imperial Theater in the Empire State." Page 13 in *The Saratoga Performing Arts Center Program Magazine* [1969 season]. Albany, New York: Showbill, 1969.

197

"The School of American Ballet: 1934–1970." Pages 3–7 in *School of American Ballet* [catalogue, 1970/1971].

198

"On Choreography" [extract from *Movement & Metaphor* (56)]. Pages 15–18, 33, 34, 37, 38–39 in *New York State Theater Magazine 5* (Nov. 17–Dec. 6, 1970) [program]. New York: Publishing Division of Metromedia, 1970. Illustrated.

199

The New York City Ballet 1946–1971 (1934–1980). [New York: New York City Ballet, 1971.] [4] pages. Illustrated.

200

"Stravinsky and Balanchine: Fifty Years of Partnership, 1920–1971." Pages [2–3] in *New York City Ballet* [souvenir program, 1971]. New York: Program Publishing Company, 1971. Illustrated.

201

"Celebration" and "Agon." Pages [5–6], [12–13] in *New York City Ballet: Igor Stravinsky, June 18, 1882–April 6, 1971* [souvenir program of the Stravinsky Festival, June 18–25, 1972]. New York: New York City Ballet, 1972.
   a. Partially reprinted (titled "On Stravinsky"), page 37, in *New York Review of Books* 18:12 (June 29, 1972). Illustrated.
   b. Reprinted (titled "The Occasion" and "Apollo : Orpheus : Agon"), pages 9–13 and 168–171, in *The Stravinsky Festival of the New York City Ballet*, written and edited by Nancy Goldner, with photographs by Martha Swope and others. New York: Eakins Press, 1973.

202

"Bemerkungen zur Geschichte des New York City Ballet."
Pages [2–7] in *Münchner Festspiele . . . 1972: Gesamtgast-
spiel New York City Ballet* [program, Aug. 11–14, 1972].
Munich: Bayerische Staatsoper, 1972. Illustrated.

    a. Reprinted (translated and revised, without illustra-
    tions, titled "New York City Ballet"), pages [17–18],
    in *The Theatregoer* (Aug. 13–25, 1973) [program,
    Greek Theatre, Los Angeles]. Hollywood: Hollywood
    Reporter, 1973.

    b. Reprinted (slightly revised), page [21], in *The Thea-
    tregoer* (Aug. 12–24, 1974). Hollywood: Hollywood
    Reporter, 1974.

203

"Melissa Hayden: 'Time to Retire?' " Pages 10, 12–13 in *The
New York State Theater Magazine* 8 (June 5–24, 1973) [pro-
gram]. New York: Publishing Division of Metromedia,
1973. Illustrated.

204

"Recollections" [extracts from *The New York City Ballet* (57)].
Pages 6–7, 9, 11–12, 17 in *New York State Theater Edition of
Playbill* 9 (Jan. 9–Feb. 17, 1974) [program]. New York:
American Theatre Press, 1974. Illustrated.

205

"The Annual Demonstrations by the School of American
Ballet." Pages 1, 8–9 in *Playbill* 11 (New York State Theater
issue, June 4–30, 1974) [program]. New York: American
Theatre Press, 1974. Illustrated.

206

"1948–1975." Pages [2–3] in *New York City Ballet* [souvenir
program, 1975]. New York: Souvenir Book Publishers, 1975.

207

"Hommage à Maurice Ravel: 1875–1975." Page [1] in *New
York City Ballet: Hommage à Ravel, 1875–1975* [souvenir

program for the performances May 14–31, 1975]. New York: Souvenir Book Publishers, 1975.

208

[Statement.] Page [2] in *School of American Ballet Tenth Annual Workshop Performances, May 21, 1975* [announcement].

209

"Evgenia Ouroussow Lehovich (1909–1975)." Pages [2–3] in *The New York City Ballet Guild Presents the Tenth Annual Workshop Performances of the School of American Ballet: Wednesday, May 21, 1975* [program]. New York: School of American Ballet, 1975. Illustrated.

210

"The Policy of a Ballet Company." Pages 3–4, 6, 9–10 in *Playbill* (New York State Theater issue, Nov. 11–30, 1975) [program]. New York: American Theatre Press, 1975.

211

"The School of American Ballet: 1934–1976." Pages 6–7 in *School of American Ballet* [catalogue, 1976/1977].

212

"Classic Ballet: Aria of the Aerial." Pages 3–4, 6, 8–9 in *Playbill* (New York State Theater issue, April 27–May 11, 1976) [program]. New York: American Theatre Press, 1976. Illustrated.

    a. Reprinted (without illustrations), pages 28–31, in *About the House* 4:12 (Summer 1976).

213

"Union Jack." Page [2] in *New York City Ballet: A Gala Performance . . . May 12, 1976* [program].

    a. Reprinted, pages 1, 3–4 (and variants), in *Playbill* (New York State Theater issue, May 13–June 27, 1976) [program]. New York: American Theatre Press, 1976. Illustrated.

b. Reprinted, pages 18–19, in *Saratoga Performing Arts Center: Saratoga Festival 1976* [program]. Albany, New York: SPAC Sales, 1976.

214

"Augustus Saint Gaudens." Page 9 in *Playbill* (New York State Theater issue, May 13–June 27, 1976) [program]. New York: American Theatre Press, 1976. Illustrated.

215

"The School of American Ballet." Pages 3–4, 6 in *Playbill* (New York State Theater issue, Nov. 16–Dec. 12, 1976) [program]. New York: American Theatre Press, 1976. Illustrated.

EXHIBITION CATALOGUES AND NOTES

216

[Statement and notes.] Pages [2–3] in *Ballet Caravan Collaborators: Julien Levy Galleries, 15 East 57th Street, New York City—December 15 to December 31.* New York: Julien Levy Galleries, [1937].

217

"Karinska: Fabergé of Costume." Pages [8–10] in *The Library & Museum of the Performing Arts at Lincoln Center Presents an Exhibition of Costumes for Opera and Ballet by Karinska: The Amsterdam Gallery, February 7 through March 18, 1967.* New York: The Library, 1967.

218

"*What* (Who?) *Is* a Fire (?) *Bird* (?)?" Pages [26–28] in *Firebird: Chagall/Karinska. An Exhibition of Ballet Costumes at the Library & Museum of the Performing Arts, The New York Public Library at Lincoln Center.* New York: The Library, [1970].

219

Dance In Sculpture: Vincent Astor Gallery, Library & Museum of the Performing Arts, The New York Public Library at Lincoln Center, February 1–April 30 1971. New York: The Library, 1971. [16] pages. Illustrated.

220

[Statement.] Pages 2–3 in *A Decade of Acquisitions: The Dance Collection 1964–1973; Vincent Astor Gallery & Dance Collection Reading Room, Performing Arts Research Center, The New York Public Library at Lincoln Center, April 9–June 2, 1973.* New York: The Library, 1973.

ON DRAWING, PAINTING,
SCULPTURE,
AND ARCHITECTURE

(From *Elie Nadelman* 1973)

Nadelman aimed at a High Style of bravura elegance and technical virtuosity based on historic absolutes. Our present taste is for low style, repudiating historicity. Pop, op, minimal, mixed-media systematically improvised, obsolescent by policy, the art of today has neither past, future, nor ambition to be compared with other art of long survival. Nadelman's craft was rooted in continuities he wished to extend, adapting rediscovery to new considerations of scale, material and use, suiting his own time, seen not as a fading year, but as one fixed date. First, he set himself an exercise of analyzing origins and succession of Western sculpture deriving from Aegean civilization, from Pheidias through the heirs of Alexander's artisans. In this pursuit he paralleled that of another East European. . . . Stravinsky, the grandest imitator in music, has noted that artists may never be more themselves than when they transform models.

Nadelman seldom vaunted himself as an original, nor was idiosyncrasy attractive until Romanticism. Few Elizabethan or Augustan poets, few baroque or rococo artists saw themselves as originators, yet personality is as apparent in poem or painting as fingerprints. Nadelman had no interest in utilizing subjective striving or neurosis. He struggled; he was no less neurotic than his neighbor, but he always presupposed capacities to do as he pleased. His pleasure was the refinement in terms of plastic form of an ordering historicity apart from and far beyond his accidental self. If he was "narcissistic" (in Freud's sense), this may be found less self-love than an adoration of tradition and craft with which he identified himself, to whose immutable logic he bore witness. . . .

His marbles are burlesque divinities, their confident bosoms stockinged over with a criss-cross, see-through reticulation suggesting skin tights of circus riders, trapeze artists, or ballet dancers. . . . Their glorified godmothers appeared in Justinian's circus alongside Theodora, a tumbler who came to be crowned empress. Their legitimate grandmothers worked for Barnum and Bailey, their mothers for Ziegfeld or Minsky. Nadelman was orchestrator of gestures, a symphonic conductor of plastic silhouettes. His statues propose standards useful in measuring the still limitless dynamics of humane virtuosity.

(*Excerpt from number 224*)

BOOKS

221

Pavel Tchelitchew Drawings. New York: H. Bittner, 1947.
22 pages, 48 plates.
   a. Reprinted by Hacker Art Books, New York, 1971.

222

Elie Nadelman Drawings. New York: H. Bittner, 1949. 53
pages, 58 plates.
   a. Reprinted by Hacker Art Books, New York, 1970.

223

The Dry Points of Elie Nadelman. New York: Curt Valentin,
1952. 11 pages, 22 matted prints.

224

Elie Nadelman. New York: Eakins Press, 1973. 359 pages.
Illustrated.

225

*Lay This Laurel: An Album on the Saint-Gaudens Memorial on
Boston Common Honoring Black and White Men Together Who
Served the Union Cause with Robert Gould Shaw and Died with
Him July 18, 1863.* With photographs by Richard Benson.
New York: Eakins Press Foundation, 1973. [83] pages.

IN BOOKS

226

"Gaudier-Brzeska, Henri." Page 71 in *Encyclopaedia Britannica*, volume 10. Chicago, 1963 and subsequent editions.

227

"Lachaise, Gaston." Page 571 in *Encyclopaedia Britannica*,
volume 13. Chicago, 1963 and subsequent editions.

228

"Nadelman, Elie." Page 58 in *Encyclopaedia Britannica*, volume 16. Chicago, 1963 and subsequent editions.

229

"Rimmer, William." Page 310 in *Encyclopaedia Britannica*, volume 19. Chicago, 1963 and subsequent editions.

230

"Introduction." Pages 9–13 in *The Art of Alex Colville*, by Helen J. Dow. Toronto: McGraw-Hill Ryerson, 1972.

ARTICLES AND REVIEWS

231

[Review of] *"Modern French Painters from 1906 to the Present Day,"* by Maurice Raynal. *Hound & Horn* 2:3 (April/June 1929), 314–315.

232

"Genius" [review of] *Savage Messiah* [Henri Gaudier-Brzeska], by H. S. Ede. *Hound & Horn* 4:3 (April/June 1931), 419–427.

233

"Jean Charlot." *Creative Art* 9:4 (Oct. 1931), 306–311. Illustrated.

234

"The Contemporary Art Society of London." *Arts Weekly* 1:6 (April 16, 1932), 123.

235

"Not Three Weeks" [letter on the Museum of Modern Art exhibition "Murals by American Painters and Photographers"]. *New Republic* 71 (No. 916, June 22, 1932), 158.

236

"Art Chronicle: Contemporary Mural Painting in the United States." *Hound & Horn* 5:4 (July/Sept. 1932), 656–663. Illustrated.

237

"Books and Characters" [on Rockefeller Center]. Boston *Evening American* (Dec. 30, 1932), 8.

238

"Philip Reisman." *Hound & Horn* 6:3 (April/June 1933), 441–444. Illustrated.

239

"Notes on Painting: Franklin Watkins." *Hound & Horn* 7:4 (July/Sept. 1934), 687–689.

240

"Drawings by Jean Charlot." *Parnassus* 7:2 (Feb. 1935), 4–5. Illustrated.

241

"An Iowa Memling" [Grant Wood exhibition at the Feragil Galleries, New York City]. *Art Front* 1:6 (July 1935), 6, 8.

242

"The Future of the Museum of Modern Art." *Direction* 2:3 (May/June 1939), 36–38.

243

"The Position of Pavel Tchelitchew." *View* 2:2 (May 1942), [12–14]. Illustrated.

244

"A Traves de un Ojo Extranjero: El Arte en Chile." *Forma: Revista de Arte* 1:5 (Oct. 1942), [1–2].

245

"Life or Death for Abstract Art? Con: A Mild Case of Cere-

brosis," by Lincoln Kirstein; "Pro: In Defense of Sensibility,"
by George L. K. Morris. *Magazine of Art* 36:3 (March
1943), 110–111, 117–119. Illustrated.

246

"Here to Stay" [on the Museum of Modern Art Latin-American exhibition]. *Town & Country* 98 (No. 4246, April 1943),
58–59, 108. Illustrated.

247

"La Reciente Obra Mural de Siqueiros en el Conjunto del
Muralismo Mexicano." *Hoy* (No. 331, June 26, 1943), 45–
57. Illustrated.

248

"Siqueiros in Chillán." *Magazine of Art* 36:8 (Dec. 1943),
282–287. Illustrated.
  a. Reprinted (revised and with variant photographs),
     pages 12–16, in *Andean Quarterly* (Winter 1944).

249

"Siqueiros: Painter and Revolutionary." *Magazine of Art* 37:1
(Jan. 1944), 22–27, 34. Illustrated.

250

"American Battle Art: 1588–1944," Part I, "Military Aids
and Operations"; II, "Portraits and Popular Myths"; III,
"Important Paintings." *Magazine of Art* 37:3; 4; 5 (March;
April; May 1944), 104–109; 146–151; 184–189. Illustrated.

251

"South American Painting" [historical survey; special con-
sideration of Candido Portinari, Lasar Segall, Horacio Butler, Pedro Figari, and others]. *Studio* 128 (No. 619, Oct.
1944), 106–113. Illustrated.

252

"Letter from France." *Magazine of Art* 38:1 (Jan. 1945), 2–7.
Illustrated.

253

"War Uncovers a Ghost of Gothic Fresco" [Priory Church of Mont St. Martin, near Longwy, France]. *Art News* 44:6 (May 1–14, 1945), 18, 31–32. Illustrated.

254

"The Quest of the Golden Lamb" [recovery of German art plunder]. *Town & Country* 100 (No. 4276, Sept. 1945), 114–115, 182–186, 189, 198. Illustrated.

255

"Rimmer Material" [letter requesting information on William Rimmer]. *Nation* 161:9 (Sept. 1, 1945), 480.

256

"Monuments of Old Germany." *Nation* 161:9 (Sept. 1, 1945), 206–207.

257

"Art in the Third Reich—Survey, 1945." *Magazine of Art* 38:6 (Oct. 1945), 223–238, 240, 242. Illustrated.

258

"Information about Dr. William Rimmer" [letter requesting information]. *New Republic* 113:19 (Nov. 5, 1945), 605.

259

"Pedro Figari." *Magazine of Art* 39:3 (March 1946), 104–107. Illustrated.
   a. Reprinted, pages [3–9], in *Pedro Figari: 1861–1938*. New York: Council for Inter-American Cooperation, 1946.

260

"Seeing Things: Mysteries of Painting" [Giovanni Bellini, Giorgione, Rembrandt, Watteau, Seurat, Picasso, Hopper, Dali]. *Mademoiselle* 23:6 (Oct. 1946), 170–171, 281–284. Illustrated.

261

"Comment" [introduction to the issue *Picasso and the Ballet, by William S. Lieberman*]. *Dance Index* 5:11/12 (Nov./Dec. 1946), 263.

262

"The Rediscovery of William Rimmer." *Magazine of Art* 40:3 (March 1947), 94–95. Illustrated.

263

"What Will History Say of Picasso." *House & Garden* 92:4 (Oct. 1947), 132–133, 216. Illustrated.

264

Elie Nadelman: Sculptor of the Dance. Issued as *Dance Index* 7:6 (1948), 129–152. Illustrated.

265

"The Interior Landscapes of Pavel Tchelitchew." *Magazine of Art* 41:2 (Feb. 1948), 49–53. Illustrated.

266

"Elie Nadelman: 1882–1946." *Harper's Bazaar* 82:8 (Aug. 1948), 132–135, 186. Illustrated.

267

"The State of Modern Painting." *Harper's Magazine* 197 (No. 1181, Oct. 1948), 47–53.
  a. Condensation, with Editor's Note, printed in *American Artist* 13:2 (Feb. 1949), 37, 66–69.

268

"The Plastic Arts: Books for Christmas" [book reviews]. *New Republic* 119:25 (Dec. 20, 1948), 24–26.

269

"The Autocratic Taste" [review of] *Aesthetics and History in the Visual Arts*, by Bernard Berenson. *New Republic* 120:2 (Jan. 10, 1949), 16–17.

270

"The Fine Arts: Public Mask and Private Sorrows" [on administrative policies of the Metropolitan Museum of Art]. *New Republic* 120:13 (March 28, 1949), 20–21.

271

"Artists and Critics: A Survey" [book reviews]. *New Republic* 120:16 (April 18, 1949), 27–29.

272

"The Fine Arts: Centrifugal, Centripetal" [review of] *Georges Braque*, by Henry R. Hope; *Georges Braque—Notebook 1917–1947; The Rise of Cubism*, by Daniel-Henry Kahnweiler. *New Republic* 120:21 (May 23, 1949), 24–26.

273

"The Fine Arts: Symbol and Device" [on ecclesiastical architecture]. *New Republic* 121:13 (Sept.26, 1949), 24–27.

274

"Art Books for Christmas" [book reviews]. *New Republic* 121:24 (Dec. 12, 1949), 25–27.

275

"Malraux's Masterpiece" [review of] *The Psychology of Art*, by André Malraux. *New Republic* 122:9 (Feb. 27, 1950), 18–19.

276

"Art Books for Christmas" [book reviews]. *New Republic* 123:24 (Dec. 11, 1950), 23–26.

277

"The Fine Arts: The Abstract Style" [book reviews]. *New Republic* 124:14 (April 2, 1951), 22.

278

"Aspects of French Taste" [review of] *The Twilight of the Absolute*, by André Malraux. *New Republic* 125:11 (Sept. 10, 1951), 18–19.

279

"Art Books for Christmas" [book reviews]. *New Republic* 125:24 (Dec. 10, 1951), 19–22.

280

[Statement on personal choice of objects for an exhibition.] Pages 42–47 in *Fourteen Eyes in a Museum Storeroom.* Issued as *University of Pennsylvania Museum Bulletin* 16:3 (Feb. 1952). Illustrated.

281

The Craft of Horace Armistead. Issued as *Chrysalis* 10:1/2 (1957). 19 pages. Illustrated.

282

"Alex Colville." *Canadian Art* 15:3 (Aug. 1958), 216–219, with French translation, 244. Illustrated.

283

"Color and Integrity: Art Books" [book reviews]. *Nation* 187:20 (Dec. 13, 1958), 456–459.

284

"The Arts from Japan" [book reviews]. *Nation* 188:5 (Jan. 31, 1959), 106–107.

285

"Arts and Monuments" [book reviews]. *Nation* 189:20 (Dec. 12, 1959), 445–448, 450–451.

286

"Art Books of the Season," Parts I and II [book reviews]. *Nation* 191:21; 22 (Dec. 17; 24, 1960), 482–486; 508–510.

287

"Architecture" [on Philip Johnson's Munson-Williams-Proctor Institute in Utica, and Amon Carter Museum of Western Art in Fort Worth]. *Nation* 192:20 (May 20, 1961), 443–446.

288

"The Art of Rackham" [review of] *Arthur Rackham: His Life and Work,* by Derek Hudson. *Nation* 193:1 (July 1, 1961), 16–17.

289

"The Glory of Chinese Art" [on the Metropolitan Museum of Art exhibition from the former Chinese Imperial collections]. *Nation* 193:11 (Oct. 7, 1961), 230–231.

290

"Rembrandt and the Bankers" [on the purchase of Rembrandt's "Aristotle Contemplating the Bust of Homer" by the Metropolitan Museum of Art, and the finances and politics of cultural institutions and publishing houses]. *Nation* 193:20 (Dec. 9, 1961), 474–475.

291

"Art Books of 1961," Parts I and II [book reviews]. *Nation* 193:21; 22 (Dec. 16; 23, 1961), 493–495; 515–518.

292

"The Wealth of the Orient" [review of books on Near and Far Eastern art]. *Nation* 194:4 (Jan. 27, 1962), 83–85.

293

"A Collection of Shakespearian Pictures at Stratford, Connecticut: 1956–61." *Shakespeare Quarterly* 13:2 (Spring 1962), 257–258. Illustrated.

294

"Pavel Tchelitchew: An Unfashionable Painter." *Show* 4:3 (March 1964), 22, 26. Illustrated.

295

"Art Books of 1964," Parts I, II, III [book reviews]. *Nation* 199:19; 20; 21 (Dec. 14; 21; 28, 1964), 470–472; 502–503; 519–522.

296
"Art Books of 1970," Parts I and II [book reviews]. *Nation* 211:21; 22 (Dec. 21; 28, 1970), 663–664, 666–667; 695, 698.

297
"Artist and/or Illustrator" [review of] *The Wyeths by N. C. Wyeth: The Intimate Correspondence of N. C. Wyeth 1901–1945*, edited by Betsy James Wyeth. *Nation* 214:4 (Jan. 24, 1972), 120–122.

298
"'Sheer Miracle to the Multitude'" [review of] *Prints and People: A Social History of Printed Pictures*, by A. Hyatt Mayor. *Nation* 214:7 (Feb. 14, 1972), 219–220.

299
"Grab the Seventh Avenue Express to Brooklyn" [review of the Brooklyn Museum exhibition "A Century of American Illustration"]. New York *Times* (April 9, 1972), section 2, page 25.

300
"A. Hyatt Mayor." *Print Review* 6 (1976), 5–11. Illustrated.

MUSEUM AND GALLERY
CATALOGUES AND NOTES

301
"Note" [unsigned]. Page [4] in *An Exhibition of the School of Paris, 1910–1928: March 20 to April 12, 1929.* Cambridge, Massachusetts: Harvard Society for Contemporary Art, 1929.

302
[Notes on the artists, unsigned.] Passim in [*Derain, Matisse, Picasso, Despiau:*] *November Seventh to Twenty-second.* Cambridge, Massachusetts: Harvard Society for Contemporary Art, [1929].

On Art

303

"Historical Background" [and notes on the artists; unsigned].
Page [2] and passim in *Modern German Art: April 18th
through May 10th, 1930*. Cambridge, Massachusetts: Harvard Society for Contemporary Art, 1930.

304

"Introductory Note" [unsigned]. Page [2] in *Exhibition of
American Folk Painting in Connection with the Massachusetts
Tercentenary Celebration: October 15 to 31, 1930*. Cambridge,
Massachusetts: Harvard Society for Contemporary Art, 1930.

305

"Introductory Note" [and notes on the photographers; unsigned]. Page [2] and passim in *Photography 1930: November 7 to 29*. Cambridge, Massachusetts: Harvard Society for
Contemporary Art, 1930.

306

"Introduction" [and notes on the artists; unsigned]. Pages
[2–4] and passim in *Bauhaus: 1919–1923, Weimar; 1924,
Dessau—December 1930–1931 January*. Cambridge, Massachusetts: Harvard Society for Contemporary Art, 1930.
   a. Reprinted (titled "Bauhaus: Introductory Note"),
      pages [3–5], in *Bauhaus: 1919–1923, Weimar; 1924,
      Dessau—January 10 to February 10*. New York: John
      Becker Gallery, [1931].
   b. Reprinted (titled "Bauhaus: Introductory Note"),
      pages [3–5], in *Catalogue of an Exhibition from the
      Bauhaus, Dessau [sic], Germany: March 13 to March 28,
      1931*. Chicago: The Arts Club of Chicago, 1931.

307

"Introductory Note" [and notes on the artists; unsigned].
Pages [2–3] and passim in *England, Ireland, Scotland, Wales,
1890–1930: Painting, Drawing, Sculpture—March 27 through
April 18, 1931*. Cambridge, Massachusetts: Harvard Society
for Contemporary Art, 1931.

308

"Mural Painting." Pages 7–11 in *Murals by American Painters and Photographers*. New York: Museum of Modern Art, 1932.
  a. Reprinted in *American Art of the 20's and 30's*. New York: Arno Press, for the Museum of Modern Art, 1969. Original paginations retained.

309

"Gaston Lachaise: His Life." Pages 7–19 in *Gaston Lachaise: Retrospective Exhibition, January 30–March 7, 1935, The Museum of Modern Art*. New York: The Museum, 1935. Illustrated.
  a. Partially reprinted, pages 31–32, in *The Sculpture of Gaston Lachaise*, with an essay by Hilton Kramer and appreciations by Hart Crane and others. New York: Eakins Press, 1967.
  b. Reprinted in *Five American Sculptors*. New York: Arno Press, for the Museum of Modern Art, 1969. Original paginations retained.

310

[Statement in the catalogue of an exhibition of the work of Jean Charlot at the John Levy Gallery, New York City, February–March 1936.]

311

[Statement.] Page [2] in *Twelve Sculptors*. New York: Bonestell Gallery, [1940].

312

"Introduction." Pages 7–8 in *American Realists and Magic Realists*, edited by Dorothy C. Miller and Alfred H. Barr, Jr., with statements by the artists. New York: Museum of Modern Art, 1943.

313

The Latin-American Collection of the Museum of Modern Art. New York: The Museum, 1943. 110 pages. Illustrated.

314

American Battle Painting, 1776–1918. Washington, D.C.: National Gallery of Art, Smithsonian Institution; New York: Museum of Modern Art, 1944. 59 pages. Illustrated.

315

William Rimmer, 1816–1879: Whitney Museum of American Art, New York, November 5–27, 1946; Museum of Fine Arts, Boston, January 7–February 2, 1947. [New York?], 1946. [44] pages. Illustrated.
   a. Introductory essay reprinted (titled "William Rimmer: His Life & Art"), pages 685–716, in *Massachusetts Review* 2:4 (Summer 1961). Illustrated.

316

"Gaston Lachaise." Pages 3–7 in *Gaston Lachaise 1882–1935: Exhibition January 20–February 15, 1947.* New York: M. Knoedler, 1947.

317

The Sculpture of Elie Nadelman. New York: Museum of Modern Art in collaboration with the Institute of Contemporary Art, Boston, and the Baltimore Museum of Art, 1948. 64 pages. Illustrated.
   a. Reprinted in *Five American Sculptors.* New York: Arno Press, for the Museum of Modern Art, 1969. Original paginations retained.

318

[Introduction.] Pages 5–16 in *Pavel Tchelitchew: Pinturas y Dibujos 1925–1948,* translated by María Rosa Oliver. Buenos Aires: Instituto de Arte Moderno, August 1949.

319

"Henry McBride." Pages [7–30] in *To Honor Henry McBride: An Exhibition of Paintings, Drawings and Water Colours, November 29–December 17, 1949.* New York: M. Knoedler Galleries, 1949.

a. Reprinted (titled "A Quasi-Preface: Henry McBride"), pages 3–16, in *The Flow of Art: Essays and Criticisms of Henry McBride*, selected, with an introduction, by Daniel Catton Rich. New York: Atheneum, 1975.

320

[Statement.] Pages [2–3] in *Symbolic Realism: April 3rd to 22nd, 1950*. New York: Edwin Hewitt Gallery, 1950.

321

"Drawings by John Wilde" [unsigned]. Pages [2–3] in *Drawings by John Wilde: May 15th thru June 3rd, 1950, Edwin Hewett Gallery*. New York: The Gallery, 1950.

322

"American Symbolic Realism." Pages 3–6 in *Symbolic Realism in American Painting 1940–1950: July 18–August 18, 1950*. London: Institute of Contemporary Arts, 1950.

323

[Statement.] Page 11 in *Kobashi: Recent Sculpture by Yasuhide Kobashi at Allan Stone, 18 East 82nd Street, New York City, March 1st–25th, 1961*. New York: Allan Stone, 1961.

324

"Pavel Tchelitchew." Pages 7–47 in *Pavel Tchelitchew: An Exhibition in the Gallery of Modern Art, 20 March through 19 April 1964*. New York: The Gallery, 1964. Illustrated.

325

"Foreword." Page [3] in *First Exhibition: James Wyeth; Paintings—November 29–December 23, 1966, M. Knoedler & Co.* New York: M. Knoedler, 1966.

326

"The Taste of Napoleon." Pages 7–30 in *The Taste of Napoleon: A Loan Exhibition Sponsored by the Society of Fellows, William Rockhill Nelson Gallery of Art, Mary Atkins Museum*

of Fine Arts, October 2, 1969–November 16, 1969. Issued as
The Nelson Gallery and Atkins Museum Bulletin 4:10 (1969).

327

"Newell Convers Wyeth 1882–1945." Pages [1–2] in *N. C. Wyeth.* Chadds Ford, Pennsylvania: Brandywine River Museum, [1972].

328

"Yasuhide Kobashi." Pages [5–6] in *The Dance: Similes & Metaphors—Kobashi.* New York: The Library & Museum of the Performing Arts—The New York Public Library at Lincoln Center, [1972].

ON PHOTOGRAPHY

(From "Walt Whitman & Thomas Eakins:
A Poet's and a Painter's Camera-Eye" 1972)

From its inception, photography offered itself as a universal facility, a ready-made skill, even an instant art, with which science had endowed the commonality through the triumph of industrial revolution. Any ordinary man could not paint a picture which would be a recognizable replica of fractional nature. All men, by snapping a shutter, could be left with fragments of time, spaced and placed, which might serve as vivid promptings to memory. The fallacy, as with most optimistic democratic absolutes, is that few men have more than listless energy or vision; and this apathy is deep, endemic—the prime stuff upon which politicians, bankers, lawyers and the police thrive. But the promise, precision and promiscuity of the camera's eye as a metaphorical attitude emboldened both Whitman's and Eakins' moral strength and artistic style. A taken picture in the fact of its taking in no way guarantees quality or significance. The poet's interminable catalogues may read like an album of tour-snapshots, a memorybook, but among his massive generalizings are to be found astonishingly particularized intaglios. Finally, it is not the perfection of mastered photographic technique in an exquisite control of light, clean printing or coherent surface which establishes the few memorable images. What sticks is not perfect facture but penetration.

The paint quality of Eakins is often dry, harsh, unappetizing compared to the cosmetic or comestible surfaces of coeval French Impressionist art, in which the

Philadelphian had absolutely no interest. Whitman's metrics in his grandest odes are by no means naive or negligible, but as a master of virtuoso rhythm or cadence he can hardly be compared to Tennyson who much admired him, or Father Hopkins who so feared and envied him. Yet, in the end Eakins' two collective portraits of the clinicians Gross and Agnew are more powerful than any comparable European work since Rembrandt. Whitman's burial-hymn for President Lincoln is a more deeply sonorous lament than the Laureate's strophes for Arthur Hallam or the Iron Duke; one must return to the King James testaments for more authority in verbal exaltation.

The superiority of our greatest painter and that of our greatest poet (who, from the testimony of *Specimen Days*, may also stand as our finest prose-master) derives in part from their visual apparatus, which in both cases was a sort of stop-motion, moving-picture or retinal mechanism, a super-camera long before the cinema's scope was universalized as a dominant idiom. Whitman made use of the physical apparatus in all its potential immediacy and candid intimacy as a public relations device to advertise the Song of His Self. Eakins handled the camera as one more tool, similar to his researches in color, perspective or gross anatomy, for shape, placement and formal composition. For them, photography had a physical and metaphysical importance in the development of parallel if separate attitudes towards an objectified, exteriorized, "realistic" world. Both men were intensely private, secret operators. Although they appeared to the daily world as being in it, they were never of it. The camera was their impersonal friend, sly collaborator and shrewd corroborator, which they made use of according to their needs.

(*Excerpt from number 340*)

IN BOOKS

329

"Photography in the United States." Pages 84–90 in *Art in America in Modern Times*, edited by Holger Cahill and Alfred H. Barr, Jr. New York: Reynal & Hitchcock, 1934. Illustrated.

330

"Photographs of America: Walker Evans." Pages 189–198 in *Walker Evans: American Photographs*. New York: Museum of Modern Art, 1938.

    a. Reprinted, pages 187–195, in *Walker Evans: American Photographs*. New York: Museum of Modern Art, [revised edition, 1962].

    b. Reprinted, pages 183–192, in *Walker Evans: American Photographs*. New York: East River Press, 1975.

331

"Henri Cartier-Bresson: Documentary Humanist." Pages 7–11 in *The Photographs of Henri Cartier-Bresson*, texts by Lincoln Kirstein and Beaumont Newhall. New York: Museum of Modern Art, 1947.

332

"Henri Cartier-Bresson." Pages [3–10] in *Photographs by Cartier-Bresson*, with introductions by Lincoln Kirstein, Beaumont Newhall. New York: Grossman, 1963.

333

"Foreword" and "A Note on the Photographer." Pages 5–11 and 53–55 in *The Hampton Album: 44 Photographs by Frances B. Johnston from an Album of Hampton Institute*. New York: Museum of Modern Art, 1966.

334

"W. Eugene Smith—Success or Failure: Art or History." Pages [127–141] in *W. Eugene Smith: His Photographs and*

Notes. New York: Aperture, 1969. Issued as *Aperture* 14:3 and 4, and separately as a Special Museum of Modern Art Edition.

ARTICLES AND REVIEWS

335
"Exhibition Notes: Photography" [Man Ray, Moholy-Nagy, Edward Weston, Alfred Stieglitz, George Platt Lynes, and others]. *Arts Weekly* 1:2 (March 18, 1932), 27–28.

336
"Comment" [introduction to the issue *Cecil Beaton*]. *Dance Index* 5:8 (Aug. 1946), 183.

337
"Artist with a Camera" [Henri Cartier-Bresson]. *New York Times Magazine* (Feb. 2, 1947), 12–13. Illustrated.

338
"The Scope of Photography" [review of] *Picture History of Photography*, by Peter Pollack; *Masters of Modern Photography*, edited by Beaumont and Nancy Newhall; *U.S. Camera 1959*, edited by Tom Maloney; *Once upon a City*, edited by Grace Mayer. *Nation* 188:16 (April 18, 1959), 347–349.

339
"Metaphors of Motion" [review of] *Cartier-Bresson's France: 285 Photographs by Henri Cartier-Bresson*, text by François Nourissier. *Nation* 212:11 (March 15, 1971), 345–346.

340
"Walt Whitman & Thomas Eakins: A Poet's and a Painter's Camera-Eye." *Aperture* 16:3 (1972), [38-64]. Illustrated.

341
"Aid and Comfort to Eakins" [review of] *The Photographs of*

Thomas Eakins, by Gordon Hendricks. *Nation* 214:20 (May 15, 1972), 630–632.

342

"The United States of Henri Cartier-Bresson." Pages 4–6 in *Coup d'Oeil Américain*, by Henri Cartier-Bresson. Issued as *Camera* 1976:7 (July 1976).

EXHIBITION NOTES

343

[Statement.] Pages [2–3] in *George Platt Lynes: Portraits (1931–52); July 15–August 28, 1960, The Art Institute of Chicago Gallery of Photography*. Chicago: The Art Institute, 1960.

344

"Richard Benson." Pages [3–4] in *Richard Benson: An Exhibition of Palladium Prints, October 6–October 30, 1976*. New York: Washburn Gallery, 1976.

ON FILM

(From "Marilyn Monroe: 1926–1962" 1962)

The death of someone who has given you intense pleasure, even if you never met, amounts almost to the
death of a personal friend. . . . Extravagant claims need
not be made for [Marilyn Monroe's] capacities as the
complete actress; she never had the chance to develop
them. But as a classic comedienne of grace, delicacy and
happy wonder, she certainly has had no peer since Billie
Burke or Ina Claire. The lightness, justness and rhythm
in her clowning often held hints of something more pen-
etrating. Her comic tone was sometimes disturbingly
ironic; her personal style was more lyric than naturalis-
tic. Irony and lyricism are two prime components of the
grand manner. . . .

In our time, who could have encompassed her character? [Not Tennessee Williams, not Brecht, not
O'Neill.] However, there is one playwright . . . far
more "modern" than many now living in the flesh.
Oscar Wilde might have triumphed with Marilyn Monroe's material, since it was so much like his own. . . .
[Wilde was] a marvelously funny, generous, profoundly
decent man, who in his whole short life (he died at forty-
six) never harmed a living soul, save himself, the wife
he adored and the two very young children who meant
more to him than anything in the world. His personal
tragedy is certainly one of the most terrible and moving
about which we have absolutely complete information.
And he was a performing artist in his public as well as in
his private life. Monroe was a woman of considerable
importance and Wilde would have known, as few others,

just wherein her importance lay. She belongs in the fairly large company of tragedians in life who also performed for money in a broader theatre. . . . Like Wilde, she often reserved her talent for her art and her genius for her life. . . .

Marilyn Monroe's life was not a waste. She gave delight. She was a criterion of the comic in a rather sad world. Her films will continue to give delight, and it is blasphemy to say she had no use. Her example, our waste of her, has the use of a redemption in artists yet untrained and unborn.

(*Excerpt from number 361*)

ARTICLES AND REVIEWS

345

"Films: *The Road to Life*" [Soviet film]. *Arts Weekly* 1:1 (March 11, 1932), 13–14. Illustrated.

346

"Films: The News Reels." *Arts Weekly* 1:2 (March 18, 1932), 35.

347

"Films: Experimental Films" [Fernand Léger, Man Ray, Lynn Riggs, Jay Leyda, Miguel Covarrubias, and others]. *Arts Weekly* 1:3 (March 26, 1932), 52, 62. Illustrated.

348

"Film Chronicle: James Cagney and the American Hero." *Hound & Horn* 5:3 (April/June 1932), 465–467. Illustrated.
    a. Reprinted in *Hound & Horn: Essays on Cinema.* New York: Arno Press, 1972. Original paginations retained.

349

"Films: The Average" [*Hell Divers* with Clark Gable and Wallace Beery; *Tempest* with Emil Jannings; *Jean de la Lune* with Madeleine Renaud and Michel Simon; the Soviet films *Cossacks of the Don* and *The Red Commander's Bride*]. *Arts Weekly* 1:4 (April 2, 1932), 78.

350

"Films" [Arnold Franck's *Avalanche* with Sepp Rish; *The Crowd Roars* with James Cagney and Joan Blondell; Johnny Weismuller as Tarzan]. *Arts Weekly* 1:5 (April 9, 1932), 102. Illustrated.

351

"Films" [Ernst Lubitsch's *One Hour with You* with Maurice Chevalier; *Der Raub der Mona Lisa*; Eisenstein's *Romance Sentimentale*]. *Arts Weekly* 1:6 (April 16, 1932), 131. Illustrated.

352
"Films: *Grand Hotel*" [Greta Garbo, John Barrymore]. *Arts Weekly* 1:7 (April 23, 1932), 149–150. Illustrated.

353
"Films: *Que Viva Méjico!*" [Eisenstein]. *Arts Weekly* 1:8 (April 30, 1932), 176, 178–179. Illustrated.

354
"Films: Movie Magazines." *Arts Weekly* 1:9 (May 7, 1932), 198–199, 201–202.

355
"Books and Characters" [review of *Grand Hotel, The Wet Parade* and *The Congress Dances*]. Boston *Evening American* (May 27, 1932), 17.

356
"Dancing in Films." *New Theatre* 3:9 (Sept. 1936), 11–13. Illustrated.

357
"TAC Magazine" [review of the magazine of the Theatre Arts Committee]. *Films* 1:1 (Nov. 1939), 111–112.

358
"Film Problems of the Quarter: History in American Films— *Gone with the Wind*" [John Ford, Marcel L'Herbier, Anatole Litvak, Max Glass, Eisenstein, and others]. *Films* 1:2 (Spring 1940), 61–67.

359
"Comment" [editors' note]. *Films* 1:2 (Spring 1940), 95–97.

360
"French Films during the Occupation." *Museum of Modern Art Bulletin* 12:3 (Jan. 1945), 16–20. Illustrated.

361

"Marilyn Monroe: 1926–1962." *Nation* 195:4 (Aug. 25, 1962), 70–73.

362

"War and Peace" [letter on Robert Hatch's review of the Soviet film version of Tolstoy's novel]. *Nation* 206:22 (May 27, 1968), 682.

363

"Movie Review" [letter on Vanessa Redgrave's performance in Karel Reisz' *The Loves of Isadora*]. *Life* 66:18 (May 9, 1969), 24A.

ON MUSIC AND DRAMA

(From "Igor Stravinsky" 1957)

The core of genius is not easy to fix, even with the advantages of historical perspective. When a man is still creating compositions of unrelieved novelty, even after fifty years, it becomes more difficult. Hardest of all is to try to specify the quality of gifts like Stravinsky's, which, while they have developed with relentless logic over the half-century, seem more akin to quicksilver than to the oaken trunks with which it is more comfortable to associate absolute prestige. Stravinsky has always resisted canonization. . . . His mind is too active, restless, sharp to make comfort for a solid cult. An acetylene torch is bright and cuts steel but it does not glow like a domestic hearth. Stravinsky has never been captured by his myth or his critics. In his life, as in his art, he is a realist—possibly a lyric-realist, but with a working intelligence so devoid of self-deception that he repels the benevolent sunset which crowns other mellow careers. Thorns protect him. . . .

Anxiety, tension, discord, dislocation, instability, aggression and hysteria he has had to dominate as has everyone else who survives the times. Instead of permitting history to plunge him, as a sensitive being of consummate gifts, into a predictable (however powerfully expressed) self-pity, romantic apology or elegant nostalgia, he has seized the most disturbing and destructive aspects of his epoch and imposed on them an order which adjudicates between the anxious present and serenity with almost prophetic austerity. The pre-atomic assault of *The Rite of Spring* seems today, forty-

five years after its inception, to relate far more to what
has happened in the world since 1913, than to "pictures
of pagan Russia." Stravinsky's unique ability to dis-
associate accepted rhythmic formulae; his superimposi-
tion of levels of syncopation with a metrical over-drive
based on formal structure; his drawn hair-wire delicacy
in separating color and quality of instrumental choirs,
give his work the final tight twist of fierce insistence
which always makes for stubborn and exacerbating
novelty.

Stravinsky has done something else which perhaps
only workers in other fields of the arts fully appreciate.
In painting, surface transparency and devotion to objec-
tive delineation, which composed a Grand Style for
more than five hundred years, has been overthrown in
two generations by a coarse, permissive, idiosyncratic
expressionism, rooted in self-pity and ostentation; in
sculpture, stone-cutting has been abandoned for a superficial linear embroidery in three dimensions; in architecture, honorific or monumental splendor has been reduced to the economy of more or less elegant rentable
space; in prose literature, visual or aural journalism has
swamped the novel and the drama. It is in music, and in
music alone, that the accumulation of almost a millen-
nium of usable tradition has been preserved for present
and future practice, as in the compositions of Stravinsky.

(*Excerpt from number 378*)

IN BOOKS

364

"Those Remarkable Russians." Pages 1–15 in *Post-Caviar: Barnstorming with Russian Grand Opera*, edited by Merle Armitage. New York and Toronto: Longmans, Green, 1939.

365

"On Producing 'A Midsummer Night's Dream.' " Pages 16–27 in *A Midsummer Night's Dream*, by William Shakespeare, edited by Charles Jasper Sisson. New York: Dell, 1960. (The Laurel Shakespeare)

ARTICLES AND REVIEWS

366

"Theatre Chronicle: *Hamlet, Mourning Becomes Electra*." *Hound & Horn* 5:2 (Jan./March 1932), 278–282.

367

"Books and Characters" [review of *Mozart*, by Marcia Davenport]. Boston *Evening American* (April 8, 1932), 25.

368

"Books and Characters" [review of *The Stage Is Set*, by Lee Simonson]. Boston *Evening American* (Dec. 16, 1932), 10.

369

"A Visit to Manuel de Falla." New York *Herald Tribune* (Oct. 12, 1941), section 6, pages 6–7.

370

"Drama: 'The Furies' at Fordham" [Aeschylus' *Eumenides*]. *Nation* 154:14 (April 4, 1942), 405–406.

371

"Repertory: Policy for the Repeatable" [New York City Opera]. *Center* 1:3 (April/May 1954), 2–5. Illustrated.

[121]

372

"Stratford on Another Avon: Canada's Shakespeare Festival." *Center* 1:5 (Aug./Sept. 1954), 6–8. Illustrated.

373

"Menotti: The Giants in Bleecker Street." *Center* 1:7 (Dec. 1954), 3–8. Illustrated.

374

"Shakespeare and the Theatre of Style." *Center* 2:2 (April 1955), 12–16. Illustrated.

375

"Shakespeare Festival Theater" [letter on the American Shakespeare Theatre, Stratford, Connecticut]. *Nation* 181:8 (Aug. 20, 1955), 164.

376

"The Future of American Opera." *Atlantic Monthly* 199:3 (March 1957), 50–55.

377

"Pictures from an Album." *High Fidelity* 7:6 (June 1957, Stravinsky Seventy-fifth Birthday Issue), 36–41. Illustrated.

378

"Igor Stravinsky." *Nation* 184:24 (June 15, 1957), 530–533.

379

"Letter from Canada" [Stratford, Ontario, Shakespeare Festival]. *Nation* 185:13 (Oct. 26, 1957), 288–290.

380

"Aristocrat of the Theatre" [review of] *The Theatre of Robert Edmond Jones*, edited and with a chronology by Ralph Pendleton. *Nation* 186:12 (March 22, 1958), 260–261.

381

"About Japan's Grand Kabuki." New York *Herald Tribune* (May 29, 1960), section 4, pages 1–2. Illustrated.

382

"Purity through the Will" [review of] *Memories and Commentaries*, by Igor Stravinsky and Robert Craft. *Nation* 191:11 (Oct. 8, 1960), 233–234.

383

"First Night in Minneapolis" [review of the opening productions of the Tyrone Guthrie Theatre, *Hamlet* and Molière's *The Miser*]. *Nation* 196:21 (May 25, 1963), 437–438.

384

[Review of] *"Music and Musical Life in Soviet Russia: 1917–1970*, by Boris Schwarz." *New York Times Book Review* (April 16, 1972), 7, 16, 18. Illustrated.

PROGRAM AND OTHER NOTES

385

"Foreword." Pages [5–9] in *Kabuki*, designed and directed by Karl Leabo. New York: Program Publishing Company, 1960.

386

[*Bunraku.* New York: Dunetz and Lovett, 1966. 24 pages. Illustrated.]

ON LITERATURE,
HISTORY, POLITICS,
AND OTHER SUBJECTS

(Epigraphs chosen to introduce chapters of
Elie Nadelman 1973)

PYTHAGORAS (DIOGENES LAERTIOS) VIII: 22–5

The principle of all things is the monad, or unit; arising from this monad the undefined dyad or two serves as material substratum to the monad, which is cause; from the monad and undefined dyad spring numbers; from numbers, points; from points, lines; from lines, plane figures; from plane figures, solid figures; from solid figures, sensible bodies, the elements of which are four, fire, water, earth and air; these elements interchange and turn into one another completely, and combine to produce a universe, animate, intelligent, spherical, with the earth at its centre, the earth itself being, too, spherical.

W. H. AUDEN (1969)

Blessed are all metrical rules that forbid automatic
    response,
Force us to choose second thoughts, free from the
    fetters of self.

NIETZSCHE CONTRA WAGNER: 1888

How the theatrical scream of passion now hurts our ears, how strange to our taste the whole romantic uproar and tumult of the senses have become, which the educated rabble loves, and all its aspirations after the elevated, inflated, and exaggerated! No, if we who have recovered still need art, it is another kind of art—a mocking, light, fleeting, divinely untroubled, divinely artificial art, which, like a pure flame, licks into unclouded skies . . . Oh, those Greeks! They knew how to live. What is required for that is to stop courageously at the surface, the fold, the skin, to adore appearance, to believe in forms, tones, words, in the whole Olympus of appearance. Those Greeks were superficial—*out of profundity.*

PARACELSUS

Imagination is like the sun, whose light is not tangible, but which can set fire to a house. Imagination leads the life of man. If he thinks of fire, he is set on fire; if he thinks of war, he wages war. All depends only on the will of man to be the sun; that is—entirely what he wishes to be.

(*Epigraphs from number 224*)

IN BOOKS

387

"Gratitude from an Advisee: S.F.D. 1926." Pages 19–20 in *A Birthday Garland for S. Foster Damon: Tributes Collected in Honor of His Seventy-fifth Birthday, February 22, 1968*, edited by Alvin Hirsch Rosenfeld and Barton Levi St. Armand. Providence, Rhode Island: Brown University, 1968.

388

[Introduction.] Pages [3–10] in *From an Album of Autograph Tributes Honoring W. McNeil Lowry for His Unique Services to the Humanities and the Arts: The Ford Foundation, October 1953–December 1974*. New York: [Eakins Press Foundation], 1975.

389

"Postscript: Wystan at War." Pages 130–133 (with "Siegfriedslage," pages 128–130) in *W. H. Auden: A Tribute*, edited by Stephen Spender. New York: Macmillan, 1975.

    a. [Also issued by George Weidenfeld and Nicolson, London, 1975.]

ARTICLES AND REVIEWS

390

"Idolator of Idiosyncrasy" [review of] *William Blake*, by Osbert Burdett. *Harvard Advocate* 113:5 (Jan. 1927), 40–41.

391

[Review of] *"Astrolabe: Infinitudes and Hypocrisies*, by S. Foster Damon." *Crimson Bookshelf* 3:7 (April 11, 1927), 3–4.

392

[Review of] *"The Marionette*, by Edwin Muir." *Crimson Bookshelf* 3:8 (May 16, 1927), 4.

393

"Meanwhile" [review of] *Meanwhile: The Picture of a Lady*, by H. G. Wells. *Hound & Horn* 1:1 (Sept. 1927), 58–60.

394
"The Swell Guy" [review of] *Trinc: A Book of Poems*, by H. Phelps Putnam. *Hound & Horn* 1:2 (Dec. 1927), 164–167.

395
[Review of] *"The Oxford Book of American Verse*, chosen and edited by Bliss Carman." *Hound & Horn* 1:3 (March 1928), 278–279.

396
[Review of] *"In the Beginning*, by Norman Douglas." *Hound & Horn* 1:4 (June 1928), 377–378.

397
[Review of] *"The Exile*, edited by Ezra Pound: Number 3, Spring 1928." *Hound & Horn* 1:4 (June 1928), 382–384.

398
"Notes for an Ingenious Freshman." *Harvard Advocate* 115:1 (Oct. 1928), 28–30.

399
[Review of] *"transition: An International Quarterly for Creative Experiment*, edited by Eugene Jolas and Robert Sage: Numbers 13–14, Summer and Fall 1928." *Hound & Horn* 2:2 (Jan./March 1929), 197–198.

400
[Review of] *"Collected Poems*, by A. E. Coppard." *Hound & Horn* 2:3 (April/June 1929), 316.

401
[Review of] *"Ah the Delicate Passion*, by Elizabeth Hall Yates." *Harvard Crimson* 95:77 (May 22, 1929), 2.

402
"To Yell with Hale" [letter correcting reference to *Hound & Horn* by W. H. Hale]. *New Republic* 67 (No. 860, May 27, 1931), 48.

403

"Roughrider, Muckraker, Gangster" [review of] *The Martial Spirit: A Study of Our War with Spain*, by Walter Millis; *The Autobiography of Lincoln Steffens; The One-Way Ride: The Red Trail of Chicago Gangland from Prohibition to Jake Lingle*, by Walter Noble Burns; *Al Capone: The Biography of a Self-made Man*, by Fred D. Pasley; *Al Capone: On the Spot*, Graphic Arts Corporation; *Exposed: Stories the Papers Dare Not Print*, Exposed Publishing Company; *Dawn*, by Theodore Dreiser. *Hound & Horn* 5:1 (Oct./Dec. 1931), 147–160.

404

"Books and Characters: Authors and Publishers" [publishing politics and economics]. Boston *Evening American* (Feb. 26, 1932), 8.

405

"Books and Characters" [review of *Sand in My Shoes*, by Katharine Ripley; *Falmouth for Orders* and *By Way of Cape Horn*, by A. J. Villiers; *Once a Grand Duke*, by Grand Duke Alexander]. Boston *Evening American* (March 4, 1932), 13.

406

"Trotsky Puts Russia in New Light: History of Revolution Dispels Conception of Soviets as Bomb Tossing Peasants" [review of *History of the Russian Revolution*, by Leon Trotsky]. Boston *Evening American* (March 11, 1932), 15.

407

"Books and Characters" [review of *Black Elk Speaks*, by Black Elk as told to John G. Neihardt, and *1919*, by John Dos Passos]. Boston *Evening American* (March 18, 1932), 21.

408

"Arms and Men" [review of] *Conquistador*, by Archibald MacLeish. *Hound & Horn* 5:3 (April/June 1932), 484–492.

409

"Books and Characters" [review of *Thrust at the Sky*, by

MacKnight Black, and *Conquistador*, by Archibald MacLeish].
Boston *Evening American* (April 1, 1932), 10.

410

"Books and Characters" [on the extraordinary quality of the
commonplace]. Boston *Evening American* (April 15, 1932),
11.

411

"Books and Characters" [review of *Midsummer Night Madness*, by Seán O'Faoláin, and discussion of Edward Garnett as
publisher's reader]. Boston *Evening American* (April 22,
1932), 23.

412

"Books and Characters" [on best-seller lists, 1921–1931].
Boston *Evening American* (April 29, 1932), 10.

413

"Books and Characters" [review of *Carl Schurz*, by Claude
Moore Fuess; *The Life of Emerson*, by Van Wyck Brooks;
Convicting the Innocent, by Edwin M. Borchard, and five other
titles]. Boston *Evening American* (May 6, 1932), 25.

414

"Books and Characters" [review of *The Story of My Life*, by
Clarence Darrow]. Boston *Evening American* (May 13,
1932), 21.

415

"Books and Characters" [on the economics and sociology of
the Depression, with a review of *Lee of Virginia*, by William
E. Brooks]. Boston *Evening American* (May 20, 1932), 27.

416

"Hounds and Horns" [letter responding to Granville Hicks'
review of *Flesh Is Heir*, signed Lincoln E. Kirstein, A. Hyatt
Mayor, Bernard Bandler, II]. *New Republic* 71 (No. 912,
May 25, 1932), 48–49.

417

"Books and Characters" [review of *Modern Architecture*, by Henry Russell Hitchcock; *Modern Architects* and *The International Style: Architecture Since 1928*, by Henry Russell Hitchcock and Philip Johnson]. Boston *Evening American* (June 3, 1932), 19.

418

"Books and Characters" [review of *My Life*, by Leon Trotsky]. Boston *Evening American* (June 10, 1932), 16.

419

"Books and Characters" [review of *The Oxford History of the United States: 1787–1917*, by Samuel Eliot Morison]. Boston *Evening American* (June 24, 1932), 25.

420

"Books and Characters" [review of *Toward Soviet America*, by William Z. Foster, and *Against Revolution*, by Gilbert Seldes]. Boston *Evening American* (July 1, 1932), 11.

421

"Books and Characters" [on the Democratic National Convention in Chicago]. Boston *Evening American* (July 8, 1932), 17.

422

"Art and the Leisure Class" [letter responding to Granville Hicks' comments on *Hound & Horn,* signed Bernard Bandler, Lincoln Kirstein, A. Hyatt Mayor]. *New Republic* 71 (No. 919, July 13, 1932), 238.

423

"Books and Characters" [on war, with a review of *Jeb Stuart*, by John W. Thomason]. Boston *Evening American* (July 15, 1932), 13.

424

"Books and Characters" [review of *Bolshevism: Theory and Practice*, by Waldemar Gurian]. Boston *Evening American* (July 22, 1932), 15.

425

"Books and Characters" [review of *American Heresy*, by Christopher Hollis]. Boston *Evening American* (Aug. 5, 1932), 16.

426

"Books and Characters" [review of *Beware of Imitations!*, compiled from the records of the United States Patent Office by A. E. Brown and H. A. Jeffcott, Jr.], Boston *Evening American* (Aug. 12, 1932), 18.

427

"Books and Characters" [on the novel, and Tolstoy's *War and Peace*]. Boston *Evening American* (Aug. 26, 1932), 17.

428

"Books and Characters" [on writing for films, and the filmscript of Hemingway's *Farewell to Arms*]. Boston *Evening American* (Sept. 2, 1932), 15.

429

"Books and Characters" [on American humor, with a review of *Who's Hooey—Nitwiticisms of the Notable*, compiled by Arthur Zipser and George Novack]. Boston *Evening American* (Sept. 16, 1932), 17.

430

"Books and Characters" [review of *Liberation of American Literature*, by V. F. Calverton]. Boston *Evening American* (Sept. 30, 1932), 9.

431

"The A-minus Mind" [review of] *Challenge to Defeat*, by William Harlan Hale. *Hound & Horn* 6:1 (Oct./Dec. 1932), 161–165.

432

"Sitting Bull Good Character Even in Life, Book Reveals" [review of *Sitting Bull: Champion of the Sioux*, by Stanley Vestal]. Boston *Evening American* (Oct. 7, 1932), 16.

433

"Books and Characters" [review of *A Man Must Fight*, by Gene Tunney]. Boston *Evening American* (Oct. 14, 1932), 29.

434

"Books and Characters" [review of *The End of the World*, by Geoffrey Dennis]. Boston *Evening American* (Oct. 21, 1932), 13.

435

"Books and Characters" [review of *God's Angry Man*, by Leonard Ehrlich]. Boston *Evening American* (Oct. 28, 1932), 24.

436

"Books and Characters" [review of *The War Begins: 1909–1914*, by Mark Sullivan]. Boston *Evening American* (Nov. 4, 1932), 15.

437

"Books and Characters" [on the national election]. Boston *Evening American* (Nov. 11, 1932), 36.

438

"Books and Characters" [review of *Extraordinary Popular Delusions and the Madness of Crowds*, by Charles MacKay]. Boston *Evening American* (Nov. 25, 1932), 17.

439

"Books and Characters" [review of Homer's *Odyssey*, translated by T. E. Lawrence]. Boston *Evening American* (Dec. 9, 1932), 39.

440

"Books and Characters" [on Herman Melville]. Boston *Evening American* (Dec. 23, 1932), 10.

441

"The Canon of Death" [review of] *Death in the Afternoon*, by Ernest Hemingway. *Hound & Horn* 6:2 (Jan./March 1933), 336–341.

a. [Reprinted, pages 59–65, in *Ernest Hemingway: The Man and His Work*, edited by John K. M. McCaffery. New York: World Publishing Company, 1950.] Reissued by Cooper Square Publishers, New York, 1969.

442

"New York Letter" [E. E. Cummings, Archibald MacLeish, *Common Sense*, Uday Shan-Kar, Radio City, Fokine, Lachaise, and others]. *New English Weekly* 2:20 (March 2, 1933), 461–462.

443

"Fair Harvard" [review of] *Not to Eat, Not for Love*, by George Anthony Weller. *Saturday Review of Literature* 9:40 (April 22, 1933), 549.

444

"Virginia Letter" [Washington, D.C., Thomas Jefferson, the University of Virginia, Robert E. Lee]. *New English Weekly* 3:7 (June 1, 1933), 159–161.

445

"The Cream of the Crop" [review of] *No More Trumpets and Other Stories*, by George Milburn; *Winner Take Nothing*, by Ernest Hemingway; *The First Wife and Other Stories*, by Pearl S. Buck; *After Such Pleasures*, by Dorothy Parker; *The Best British Short Stories of 1933*, edited by Edward J. O'Brien; *A Footnote to Youth*, by José Garcia Villa. *Virginia Quarterly Review* 10:1 (Jan. 1934), 145–148.

446

" 'T. E. "Lawrence" ' " [review of] *Colonel Lawrence: The Man Behind the Legend*, by Liddell Hart. *New Republic* 78 (No. 1011, April 18, 1934), 279–280.

447

"A Century of Progress: 1833–1934" [Chicago World's Fair]. *Nation* 138 (No. 3598, June 20, 1934), 695–697.

448

"Permanence and the Present" [review of] *Before Disaster*, by

Yvor Winters, and *Horizons of Death,* by Norman Macleod.
New Republic 81 (No. 1042, Nov. 21, 1934), 53–54.

449

"Harvard and Hanfstängl" [letter on an anti-German demonstration]. *Nation* 139 (No. 3622, Dec. 5, 1934), 648–649.

450

"The Hound & Horn, 1927–1934; With a Letter from Varian Fry as a Note." *Harvard Advocate* 121:2 (Christmas 1934), 6–10, 92–94.

451

"First Poems" [review of] *Permit Me Voyage,* by James Agee, and *Avalanche of April,* by Kimball Flaccus. *New Republic* 82 (No. 1056, Feb. 27, 1935), 80–81.

452

"Death of Heroes" [review of] *Vienna,* by Stephen Spender. *Direction* 1:3 (April/June 1935), 151–152.

453

"Memoirs of a Diplomat" [review of] *The Memoirs of Sir Ronald Storrs. Nation* 145:23 (Dec. 4, 1937), 620.

454

"The English" [review of] *Helen's Tower,* by Harold Nicolson. *Nation* 146:10 (March 5, 1938), 277–278.

455

"Grass Roots" [review of] *Whitman,* by Newton Arvin. *Nation* 147:20 (Nov. 12, 1938), 513–514.

456

[Review of] "*The Letters of T. E. Lawrence,* edited by David Garnett." *Nation* 149:2 (July 8, 1939), 47–48.

457

"Poets under Fire" [review of] *Journey to a War,* by W. H. Auden and Christopher Isherwood. *Nation* 149:6 (Aug. 5, 1939), 151–152.

458

"Infra Dig" [review of] *New Directions 1940*, edited by James Laughlin, and *Twice a Year*, *V–VI*, edited by Dorothy Norman. *Accent* 1:3 (Spring 1941), 183–185.

459

"Argentine Afternoon" [visits with María Rosa Oliver and Victoria Ocampo during American Ballet Caravan South American tour]. *Town & Country* 97 (No. 4232, Jan. 1942), 34–35, 72–73. Illustrated.

460

"Poet and Prophet" [review of] *South American Journey*, by Waldo Frank. *New Republic* 108:26 (June 28, 1943), 866–867.

461

"Recent Latin American Novels" [review of] *The Bay of Silence*, by Eduardo Mallea; *Sunburst*, by Mauricio Magdaleno; *The Horse and His Shadow*, by Enrique Amorim; *The Golden Serpent*, by Ciro Alegría; *Canapé-Vert*, by Pierre Marcelin and Philippe Thoby-Marcelin. *New Republic* 110:17 (April 24, 1944), 574, 576, 578.

462

"Paris Alive: The Republic of Silence," by Jean-Paul Sartre, translated by Lincoln Kirstein. *Atlantic Monthly* 174:6 (Dec. 1944), 39–40.

463

"Letter from France." *Nation* 160:4 (Jan. 27, 1945), 102–106.

464

"A Visit to Der Stuermer" [Julius Streicher]. *Nation* 160:26 (June 30, 1945), 722–723.

465

"Presence de France" [anthology including Valéry, Max Jacob, Giraudoux, Cocteau, Gide, Mauriac, Louis Jouvet, and others], edited and translated by Lincoln Kirstein. *Sewanee Review* 53:3 (Oct. 1945), 586–608.

466

"Common Sense without Pity" [review of] *The Temple of the Golden Pavilion*, by Yukio Mishima; *Zen and Japanese Culture*, by Daisetz T. Suzuki; *Japan: Ancient Buddhist Paintings*, UNESCO World Art Series; *Beat Zen, Square Zen, & Zen*, by Alan W. Watts. *Nation* 189:4 (Aug. 15, 1959), 76–78.

467

"Echoes from a Buddhist Temple" [letter responding to Nancy Wilson Ross' objections to "Common Sense without Pity"]. *Nation* 189:16 (Nov. 14, 1959), facing 341.

468

"The New Augustan Age" [on the inauguration of President John F. Kennedy]. *Nation* 192:5 (Feb. 4, 1961), 106–108.

469

"Letter from Seattle" [Seattle World's Fair]. *Nation* 194:14 (April 7, 1962), 315–319.

470

"Carl Van Vechten (1880–1964)." *Yale University Library Gazette* 39:4 (April 1965), 156–162. Illustrated.

471

"Newbold Morris: 1902–1966." *Dance News* 48:5 (May 1966), 4. Illustrated.

472

"A Prison of Possibility" [review of] *Inside the Third Reich: Memoirs by Albert Speer*, translated by Richard and Clara Winston. *Nation* 211:7 (Sept. 14, 1970), 216–217.

473

"Marriage of Poetry and Painting" [review of] *The Illuminated Blake*, annotated by David V. Erdman. *Nation* 219:16 (Nov. 16, 1974), 503–504.

INDEX

A. Everett Austin, Jr. . . . , 67
"A. Hyatt Mayor", 300
"The A-minus Mind", 431
"A Traves de un Ojo Extranjero", 244
"About 'Billy the Kid' ", 117
"About Dancers", 120
"About Japan's Grand Kabuki", 381
About the House, 176, 178, 212
"The Abstract Style", 277
Accent, 458
"Achievement", 63
Aeschylus, 370
Agee, James, 451
'Agon', 176, 201
"Agon", 201
"Aid and Comfort to Eakins", 341
"Album of Dancers", 127
An Album of Nijinsky Photographs, 148
"Alec . . .", 66
Alegría, Ciro, 461
"Alex Colville", 282
Alexander Mikhailovich, Grand Duke of Russia, 405
American Art of the 20's and 30's, 308
American Artist, 267
American Ballet, 35, 36, 92, 95, 101, 132, 161
American Ballet Caravan, 44, 45, 142–145, 459
"The American Ballet in Argentina", 143; ". . . in Brazil", 142; ". . . in Chile", 144; ". . . on the West Coast", 145
American Ballet Theatre: *see* Ballet Theatre
"American Battle Art", 250
American Battle Painting, 314
American Dancer, 115, 142–145
The American Imagination, 169
"An American Institution Is Founded", 103
American Realists and Magic Realists, 312
"American Saturday Night", 123
American Shakespeare Theatre, 293, 375
"American Symbolic Realism", 322
Amon Carter Museum, 287
Amorim, Enrique, 461
Anna Pavlova, 150
"The Annual Demonstrations by the School of American Ballet", 205
Antheil, George, 35
Aperture, 334, 340
'Apollo', 158, 201
"Apollo : Orpheus : Agon", 201
'Apollon Musagète': *see* 'Apollo'
"Architecture", 287
"Argentine Afternoon", 459
"Aristocrat of the Theatre", 380
'Aristotle Contemplating the Bust of Homer', 290
Armistead, Horace, 281

Armitage, Merle, 61, 364
"Arms and Men", 408
"Art and the Leisure Class", 422
"Art Books for Christmas", 274, 276, 279
"Art Books of 1961", 291; ". . . of 1964", 295; ". . . of 1970", 296
"Art Books of the Season", 286
"Art Chronicle", 236
Art Front, 94, 241
Art in America in Modern Times, 329
"Art in the Third Reich", 257
Art News, 253
The Art of Alex Colville, 230
"The Art of Rackham", 288
"Arthur Bronson", 167
"Artist and/or Illustrator", 297
"Artist with a Camera", 337
"Artists and Critics", 271
Arts and Decoration, 102
"Arts and Monuments", 285
"The Arts from Japan", 284
Arts Weekly, 234, 335, 345–347, 349–354
Arvin, Newton, 455
"Aspects of French Taste", 278
Astaire, Fred, 81, 112
"Astonishing Reply", 172
Atlantic Monthly, 376, 462
Auden, W. H., 30, 389, 457
"Audience", 125
"Augustus Saint Gaudens", 214
Austin, A. Everett, Jr. ('Chick'), 67
"Authors and Publishers", 404
"The Autocratic Taste", 269
Avalanche, 350

L'Avare: see The Miser
"The Average", 349
"Away from the Home of the Ballet", 96

"Baby Gangster", 20
"Back to School", 17
Bakst, Léon, 94
Balanchine, George, 35, 36, 46, 78, 80, 86, 88, 95, 151, 158, 159, 161, 166, 168, 169, 175, 176, 200
"Balanchine and American Ballet", 161
"Balanchine and the Classic Revival", 159
"Balanchine Musagète", 158
"Balanchine Trio", 176
"Balanchine's Fourth Dimension", 175
"Ballet", 78, 132
Ballet, 161
"Ballet" [column], 104, 105, 107
Ballet Alphabet, 52, 55
Ballet & Modern Dance, 69
"Ballet and Music", 62
"Ballet and the Modern Dance Today", 98
"Ballet Blitz", 134
Ballet Caravan, 37–43, 115, 119, 124, 132, 180–183, 216
"Ballet Caravan", 182
"The Ballet Caravan", 180, 183
The Ballet Caravan [announcement, 1937/1938], 181; [January 6 and 7, 1938], 183
Ballet Caravan [prospectus,

1937?], 180; [souvenir program, 1937/1938], 182

Ballet Caravan Collaborators, 216

"Ballet Has Own Logic", 170

"The Ballet in Hartford", 67

"The Ballet Is Classic", 93

"Ballet 'Round the World", 118

Ballet Russe de Monte Carlo: *see* Monte Carlo Ballet Russe for the company founded by René Blum in 1931 and directed in partnership with Vasili de Basil until 1936; *see* Ballet Russe de Monte Carlo for the company directed by René Blum after 1936, and later by Sergei Denham and Leonide Massine; *see* Original Ballet Russe for the company directed by Vasili de Basil from 1936 to 1948

Ballet Russe de Monte Carlo, 78, 132, 134, 135, 140

Ballet Society, 46, 47, 63, 187

The Ballet Society: First Program, 187

The Ballet Society: 1946–1947, 63

Ballet Theatre, 132, 134, 141

Les Ballets 1933, 78

Bandler, Bernard, II, 416, 422

"Bar & Grill", 28

Barnes, Clive, 174

Barr, Alfred H., Jr., 312, 329

Barry and Coe, 81

Barrymore, John, 352

Barzin, Jane, 46, 187

The Bat, 36

"Bath", 31

Bauhaus, 306

Baum, Morton, 195

Beaton, Sir Cecil, 336

Beaumont, Cyril W., 113, 128

Beery, Wallace, 349

Bellini, Giovanni, 260

"Bemerkungen zur Geschichte des New York City Ballet", 202

Benois, Alexandre, 94, 174

Benson, Richard, 60, 70, 225, 344

Bérard, Christian, 86

Berenson, Bernard, 269

Berkeley, Busby, 81

Berlanga, José Martínez, 2

Bernstein, Aline, 46

Bert (photographer), 59

"Between the Bells", 17

'Billy the Kid', 117

Billy the Kid, 41

A Birthday Garland for S. Foster Damon, 387

Black, MacKnight, 409

Black Elk, 407

"Black Joe", 24

Blake, William, 390, 473

Blanc, Kyra, 155

Blast at Ballet, 51, 55

Blondell, Joan, 350

Bolger, Ray, 112, 131

The Book of the Dance, 50

"Books and Characters" [column], 237, 355, 367, 368, 404, 405, 407, 409–415, 417–421, 423–430, 433–440

Borchard, Edwin M., 413

Boston *Evening American*, 237, 355, 367, 368, 404–407, 409–

415, 417–421, 423–430, 432–440

Boston *Evening Transcript*, 118, 122, 127, 128

Bowles, Paul, 39, 147

Bowman, Patricia, 81

Brant, Henry, 43

Braque, Georges, 272

Brinson, Peter, 173

Bronson, Arthur, 167

Brooklyn Museum, 299

Brooks, Van Wyck, 413

Brooks, William E., 415

Brown, Alford E., 426

Buck, Pearl S., 445

Buck and Bubbles, 81

"A Building as a Ballerina", 192

Bunraku, 386

Burdett, Osbert, 390

Burns, Walter Noble, 403

Butler, Horacio, 251

Caccialanza, Gisella, 124

Cadmus, Paul, 40, 52

Cagney, James, 348, 350

Cahill, Holger, 329

Calder, Alexander, 94

Calverton, V. F., 430

Camera, 342

Canadian Art, 282

"The Canon of Death", 441

Capone, Al, 403

'The Card Party', 101

"Carl Van Vechten", 470

Carman, Bliss, 395

Carnaval, Le Spectre de la Rose and Les Sylphides, 49

Carter, Elliott, Jr., 38, 47

Cartier-Bresson, Henri, 331, 332, 337, 339, 342

Castle, Vernon, 112

Catalogue of an Exhibition from the Bauhaus . . . , 306

Cecil Beaton, 336

"Celebration", 201

Center, 164, 371–374

"Centrifugal, Centripetal", 272

"A Century of Progress", 447

Chabrier, Emmanuel, 86

Chabukiani, Vachtang, 80

Chaffee, George, 149

Chagall, Marc, 218

"Chamber of Horrors", 21

Chaplin, Charles, 131

Charade, 42

Charlot, Jean, 233, 240, 310

Chevalier, Maurice, 351

Christensen, Lew, 38, 40, 42, 124

Chrysalis, 281

Chujoy, Anatole, 64, 66, 68

The City Center of Music and Drama Presents the New York City Ballet at the New York State Theater . . . , 192

City Portrait, 43

"Classic Ballet: Aria of the Aerial", 212

The Classic Ballet, 65

Claudel, Paul, 48

Clowns, Elephants and Ballerinas, 156

Cocteau, Jean, 172, 465

Colette, 46, 187

"A Collection of Shakespearian Pictures . . .", 293

"Color and Integrity", 283

Colt, Alvin, 42

Colville, Alex, 230, 282
"Comment" [in *Dance Index*], 148–154, 156, 157, 261, 336
"Comment" [in *Films*], 359
Common Sense, 442
"Common Sense without Pity", 466, 467
"The Complete Whifflepink . . .", 7
The Congress Dances, 355
"The Contemporary Art Society of London", 234
"Contemporary Mural Painting . . .", 236
Copland, Aaron, 41, 45, 117
Coppard, A. E., 400
'Coppélia', 70, 179
Coppélia, 70
Cornell, Joseph, 156
"Correspondence", 84
Cossacks of the Don, 349
"'Cotillion'; 'Union Pacific'", 86
Coup d'Oeil Américain, 342
Covarrubias, Miguel, 347
Craft, Robert, 382
The Craft of Horace Armistead, 281
Crane, Hart, 309
"The Cream of the Crop", 445
Creative Art, 233
Crimson Bookshelf, 391, 392
'Crisis in the Dance", 100
The Criticism of Edwin Denby, 152
"The Critic's Lexicon", 111
The Crowd Roars, 350
Cummings, E. E., 442
Current Controversy, 93

Dali, Salvador, 260
Damon, S. Foster, 387, 391
Dance, 98, 103, 114, 119, 121, 126, 129, 135
"The Dance" [column], 80, 81, 86, 87, 89, 106, 111
"The Dance: A Letter", 92
Dance: A Short History . . . , 50
"The Dance: Repertory; Ballet Director Suggests . . .", 162
The Dance: Similes & Metaphors —Kobashi, 328
Dance and Dancers, 179
"The Dance Archives", 139
"The Dance as Theatre", 90
"Dance Chronicle", 75
Dance Collection, New York Public Library, 220; *see also* 139
"Dance Documentary", 113
The Dance Encyclopedia, 64, 68
"Dance in Review", 135
Dance in Sculpture, 219
Dance Index, 148–154, 156, 157, 261, 264, 336
"Dance International 1900–1937", 108, 109
Dance Magazine, 177
Dance News, 155, 160, 163, 165, 167, 171, 471
Dance News Annual, 66
Dance Notation, 154
Dance Observer, 84, 104, 105, 107, 109, 117, 125, 130
"The Dance of Forever", 121
"Dance through the Ages", 110
"Dancing in Films", 356
Dancing Times, 176
Darrow, Clarence, 414
Davenport, Marcia, 367

"*De Fine Mundi*", 5
"Dead on Arrival", 28
"Dear Editor", 138
Deas, Stewart, 49
"Death of Heroes", 452
The Debutante: see Charade
A Decade of Acquisitions, 220
Decision, 140, 141
"Decor and Costume", 128
De Laban, Juana, 154
Delibes, Léo, 70, 179
"Delibes and *Coppélia*", 70
De Meyer, Baron Adolphe, 59
De Mille, Agnes, 89, 151
Denby, Edwin, 59, 148, 151, 152, 193
Dennis, Geoffrey, 434
Derain, André, 302
Derain, Matisse, Picasso, Despiau, 302
Despiau, Charles, 302
Diaghilev, Sergei, 74, 78, 126, 137, 160, 165, 172
"The Diaghilev Period", 74
Direction, 242, 452
Dodge, Roger Pryor, 89
Dollar, William, 44
The Dome, 5, 6, 14, 15
Dos Passos, John, 407
Douglas, Norman, 396
Dow, Helen J., 230
"Drama: 'The Furies' at Fordham", 370
Draper, Paul, 112
"Drawings by Jean Charlot", 240
Drawings by John Wilde, 321
"Drawings of Dancers", 136
Dreiser, Theodore, 403
Druet (photographer), 59

The Dry Points of Elie Nadelman, 223
Duncan, Isadora, 77, 146, 153, 363
Dutray, Pierre, 48

Eakins, Thomas, 340, 341
Ebsen, Buddy, 81, 112, 131
Ebsen, Vilma, 81
"Eccentric Dancing", 131
"Echoes from a Buddhist Temple", 467
Ede, Harold S., 232
"Edwin Denby on the Dance", 193
Ehrlich, Leonard, 435
Eisenstein, Sergei, 27, 351, 353, 358
"Eisenstein", 27
Elie Nadelman, 224
"Elie Nadelman: 1882–1946", 266
Elie Nadelman: Sculptor of the Dance, 264
Elie Nadelman Drawings, 222
Ellmann, Richard, 31, 32
Emerson, Ralph Waldo, 413
Encyclopaedia Britannica, 226–229
L'Enfant et les Sortilèges, 46, 187
England, Ireland, Scotland, Wales, 1890–1930, 307
"The English", 454
Erdman, David V., 473
Ernest Hemingway, 441
Essays on Cinema, 348
Eumenides, 370
Evans, Walker, 152, 330

vgenia Ouroussow Lehovich", 209

xhibition Notes: Photography", 335

xhibition of American Folk Painting . . . , 304

n Exhibition of the School of Paris, 301

he Exile, 397

xperimental Films", 347

he Face of the Company", 164

air Harvard", 443

all In", 31, 32

alla, Manuel de, 369

eragil Galleries, 241

estspielhaus", 23

igari, Pedro, 251, 259

illing Station, 40

ilm Chronicle", 348

ilm Problems of the Quarter", 358

lms, 357–359

lms" [column], 345–347, 349–354

he Fine Arts" [column], 270, 272, 273, 277

rebird', 218

irebird: Chagall/Karinska, 218

rst Exhibition: James Wyeth . . . , 325

rst Night in Minneapolis", 383

rst Poems", 451

tts, Dudley, 21

ve American Sculptors, 309, 317

xer", 25

Flaccus, Kimball, 451

Flesh Is Heir, 1, 3, 416

The Flow of Art, 319

Fokine, Michel, 49, 76, 88, 138, 174, 442

Fokine, 49

For John Martin, 58

For Lincoln . . . , 3

For My Brother, 2

For W. H. Auden . . . , 30

Ford, John, 358

"Foresight", 31

Forma, 244

Foster, William Z., 420

'The Four Temperaments', 176

Fourteen Eyes in a Museum Storeroom, 280

Franck, Arnold, 350

Frank, Waldo, 460

Free, Karl, 38

French, Jared, 41

"French Films during the Occupation", 360

From an Album . . . Honoring W. McNeil Lowry . . . , 388

From Flesh Is Heir, 3

Frost, Mary, 9

Fry, Varian, 450

Fuess, Claude Moore, 413

"'The Furies' at Fordham", 370

"The Future of American Opera", 376

"The Future of the Museum of Modern Art", 242

Gable, Clark, 349

Gagaku, 54

A Gala Performance . . . , 213

Garbo, Greta, 352
"A Garden Party in Simia", 14
Garfias, Robert, 54
Garnett, David, 456
Garnett, Edward, 411
"Gaston Lachaise", 316
"Gaston Lachaise: His Life", 309
Gaston Lachaise: Retrospective Exhibition, 309
Gaston Lachaise 1882–1935, 316
Gaudier-Brzeska, Henri, 226, 232
"Gaudier-Brzeska, Henri", 226
"Genius", 232
George Balanchine, 151
"George Platt Lynes", 189
George Platt Lynes: Portraits, 343
Georges Braque — Notebook, 272
"Georgic", 19, 21
Gide, André, 465
Gilder, Rosamond, 158
Ginastera, Alberto, 147
Giorgione, 260
Giraudoux, Jean, 465
Glass, Max, 358
"The Glory of Chinese Art", 289
Goldner, Nancy, 70, 201
Goncharova, Natalia, 94
Gone with the Wind, 358
"Good Dance Book", 122
Goode, Gerald, 127
"Grab the Seventh Avenue Express to Brooklyn", 299
Graham, Martha, 61, 83, 89, 116, 124
Grand Hotel, 352, 355
"Grass Roots", 455
"Gratitude from an Advisee", 387

Guarnieri, Camargo, 147
Gurian, Waldemar, 424

Hale, William Harlan, 402, 48
Hamlet, 366, 383
The Hampton Album, 333
Hampton Institute, 333
"Happy, Happy, Happy Pair", 6
Harlequin for President, 37
Harper's Bazaar, 123, 133, 2(
Harper's Magazine, 8, 267
Harvard Advocate, 7, 16, 390, 398, 450
"Harvard and Hanfstängl", 4
Harvard Crimson, 401
Harvard Society for Contemp rary Art, 301–307
Haskell, Arnold L., 49, 118
Hatch, Robert, 362
Hayden, Melissa, 177, 203
Hemingway, Ernest, 428, 44 445
Hendricks, Gordon, 341
"Henri Cartier-Bresson", 332
"Henri Cartier-Bresson: Documentary Humanist", 331
"Henry McBride", 319
"Here to Stay", 246
Hicks, Granville, 416, 422
High Fidelity, 377
"Hijack", 24
"Historical Background", 303
"History in American Films . . 358
Hitchcock, Henry Russell, 41
Hollis, Christopher, 425
"Homage to Michel Fokine",
"Homage to Stravinsky", 102

"Home Team: The Ballet Theatre", 141

Homer, 439

"Hommage à Maurice Ravel", 207

Hommage à Ravel, 1875–1975, 187, 207

Hope, Henry R., 272

Hopper, Edward, 260

Hound & Horn, 17–19, 74, 75, 79, 231, 232, 236, 238, 239, 348, 366, 393–397, 399, 400, 402, 403, 408, 422, 431, 441, 450

Hound & Horn: Essays on Cinema, 348

"The Hound & Horn, 1927–1934", 450

"Hounds and Horns", 416

House & Garden, 263

Hoy, 247

Hudson, Derek, 288

Hudson Review, 24–26, 28

Humphries, Doris, 89

'Idolator of Idiosyncrasy", 390

'Igor Stravinsky", 378

Igor Stravinsky . . . 1882–. . . 1971, 201

'An Imperial Theater in the Empire State", 196

"Important Paintings", 250

'In Appreciation: John Martin", 171

'In Defense of Sensibility", 245

'In Defense of the Ballet", 85

'In Memoriam: Serge de Diaghileff", 126

"The Increased Popularity of Ballet in America", 178

"The Indians Dance", 133

"Information about Dr. William Rimmer", 258

"Infra Dig", 458

"The Interior Landscapes of Pavel Tchelitchew", 265

The International Cyclopedia of Music and Musicians, 62

"Introduction and Credo", 104

"Inventory", 18

"An Iowa Memling", 241

"Is Ballet Alive?", 91

"Isadora Duncan", 146

Isadora in Art, 153

Isherwood, Christopher, 457

Jacob, Max, 465

"James Cagney and the American Hero", 348

James Wyeth; Paintings, 325

Jannings, Emil, 349

"Jean Charlot", 233

Jeffcott, Harry A., Jr., 426

Jefferson, Thomas, 444

'Jeu de Cartes', 101

Joffrey Ballet, 174

Johnson, Philip, 287, 417

Johnston, Frances B., 333

Jolas, Eugene, 399

Jones, Robert Edmond, 380

Jooss, Kurt, 78

Jooss Ballet, 105

Jouvet, Louis, 465

Juke Box, 44

Junyer, Joan, 47

"K.P.", 24

Kabuki, 385

Kahnweiler, Daniel-Henry, 272

Karinska, Barbara, 217, 218

"Karinska: Fabergé of Costume",
217

Kennedy, John Fitzgerald, 468

Kenyon Review, 120

"Kirstein Argues about Petrouchka", 174

"Kirstein Blasts Open Shop", 129

"Kirstein 1937", 61

Kobashi, Yasuhide, 54, 323, 328

Kobashi: Recent Sculpture, 323

Kochno, Boris, 78

Kramer, Hilton, 309

Kreutzberg, Harald, 75

Kurashikku Baree, 65

"'Kykunkor'; Native African Opera", 87

"Kyra Blanc: In Memoriam", 155

Lachaise, Gaston, 227, 309, 316,
442

"Lachaise, Gaston", 227

'Lamentation', 124

Larionov, Mikhail, 94

Lassalle, Nancy Norman, 71, 72

*The Latin-American Collection of
the Museum of Modern Art*,
313; *see also* 246

"Latin American Music for Ballet", 147

Laughlin, James, 458

Lawrence, T. E., 439, 446, 456

Lay This Laurel, 225

Leabo, Karl, 385

Lederman, Minna, 101

Lee, Robert E., 415, 444

Lee, Tom, 44

"The Legacy of Diaghilew", 160

Léger, Fernand, 347

Lehovich, Evgenia Ouroussow,
209

Lengyel, Lydia, 48

"Léo Delibes and the Inscape of
Coppélia", 179

Le Roy, Hal, 112

"Letter from Canada", 379

"Letter from France", 252, 463

"Letter from Seattle", 469

Leyda, Jay, 347

L'Herbier, Marcel, 358

*The Library & Museum of the
Performing Arts at Lincoln
Center Presents . . . Karinska*,
217

Liddell Hart, Basil, 446

Lieberman, William S., 261

Lifar, Serge, 78, 137

"Lifar on Diaghilev", 137

Life, 363

"The Life of Byrne", 21

"Life or Death for Abstract Art?",
245

Liszt, Franz, 35

Littlefield, Catherine, 105

Litvak, Anatole, 358

Longchamp, Gaston, 35

Loring, Eugene, 37, 39, 41, 43,
117

The Loves of Isadora, 363

Low Ceiling, 11, 17–21

Lowry, W. McNeil, 388

Lubitsch, Ernst, 351

Lynes, George Platt, 57, 189,
335, 343

McBride, Henry, 319
McCaffery, John K. M., 441
Macdougall, Allan Ross, 153
MacKay, Charles, 438
MacLeish, Archibald, 86, 408, 409, 442
Macleod, Norman, 448
Mademoiselle, 260
Magazine of Art, 245, 248–250, 252, 257, 259, 262, 265
Magdaleno, Mauricio, 461
Magic Carpet, 34
"Make the Dance American", 93
Mallea, Eduardo, 461
Maloney, Tom, 338
Malraux, André, 275, 278
"Malraux's Masterpiece", 275
Manchester, P. W., 68
"The Map of Movement", 173
Marcelin, Philippe Thoby-: *see* Thoby-Marcelin, Philippe
Marcelin, Pierre, 461
"March", 29
"March from the Ruins of Athens", 16
"Marilyn Monroe", 361
Marius Petipa, 157
A Marriage Message . . . , 9
"Marriage of Poetry and Painting", 473
Martha Graham, 61
"Martha Graham at Bennington", 116
Martin, John, 58, 92, 99, 111, 163, 171
Martin, Keith, 36, 37
"Martin of *The Times*", 163
Marx Brothers, 131
Massachusetts Review, 23, 27, 29, 315

Massine, Leonide, 86, 88, 105, 131
Matisse, Henri, 302
Matsumoto, R., 65
"Maudlin Meditations", 15
Mauriac, François, 465
Maybon, James, 9
Mayer, Grace, 338
Mayor, A. Hyatt, 298, 300, 416, 422
"Meanwhile", 393
"Melissa Hayden: A Tribute", 177
"Melissa Hayden: 'Time to Retire?' ", 203
Melville, Herman, 440
"Memoirs of a Diplomat", 453
"Memorial", 22
"Memorial Window: 1946–56", 22
Menotti, Gian-Carlo, 373
"Menotti: The Giants in Bleecker Street", 373
"Metaphors of Motion", 339
Metropolitan Museum of Art, 270, 289, 290
A Midsummer Night's Dream, 365
A Midsummer Night's Dream: The Story . . . , 72
Mignone, Francisco, 147
Milburn, George, 445
"A Mild Case of Cerebrosis", 245
"Military Aids and Operations", 250
Miller, Dorothy C., 312
Millis, Walter, 403
The Minotaur, 47
Miró, Joan, 94

The Miser, 383
Mishima, Yukio, 466
"Modern Ballet", 178
" 'Modern Dance' and Dancing",
    77
Modern German Art, 303
Modern Music, 85, 101
Modern Poems, 24, 32
Moholy-Nagy, Laszlo, 335
Molière, 383
Monroe, Marilyn, 361
Mont St. Martin Priory Church,
    253
Monte Carlo Ballet Russe, 80,
    86, 97, 132
"The Monte Carlo Season", 106
"The Monument of Diaghilev",
    165
"Monuments of Old Germany",
    256
Moore, Lillian, 120
Moore, Marianne, 150
Morcom, James Stewart, 45
Mori, K., 65
Morison, Samuel Eliot, 419
Morris, George L. K., 245
Morris, Newbold, 471
Morton Baum, 195
Mourning Becomes Electra, 366
Movement & Metaphor, 56, 198
"Movie Magazines", 354
"Movie Review", 363
Mozart, Wolfgang Amadeus,
    367
Münchner Festspiele . . . 1972,
    202
Muir, Edwin, 392
Munson-Williams-Proctor Insti-
    tute, 287

"Mural Painting", 308
*Murals by American Painters and
    Photographers*, 308; *see also*
    235, 236
"A Museum of Ballet", 97
Museum of Modern Art, New
    York, 139, 235, 242, 246
Museum of Modern Art Bulletin,
    139, 146, 360
Museum of Western Art, Fort
    Worth, 287
"The Music Hall; Revues; the
    Movies", 81
The Music Lover's Handbook, 62

N. C. Wyeth, 327
Nabokov, Nicolas, 86
Nadelman, Elie, 222–224, 228,
    264, 266, 317
"Nadelman, Elie", 228
Napoleon I, 326
Nation, 22, 80–82, 86, 87, 89,
    106, 110–113, 116, 137, 172,
    255, 256, 283–292, 295–298,
    338, 339, 341, 361, 362, 370,
    375, 378–380, 382, 383, 447,
    449, 453–457, 463, 464, 466–
    469, 472, 473
"The Nature of American Bal-
    let", 169
Neihardt, John G., 407
*The Nelson Gallery and Atkins
    Museum Bulletin*, 326
"The New Augustan Age", 468
New Directions, 458
New English Weekly, 20, 76, 77,
    442, 444
New Republic, 83, 235, 258,

268–279, 402, 416, 422, 446, 448, 451, 460, 461
New Theatre, 88, 90, 97, 356
New York City Ballet, 53, 57, 69, 71–73, 161, 164, 166, 168, 169, 175, 187–189, 199–202, 204, 206, 207, 210, 213; *see also* American Ballet, American Ballet Caravan, Ballet Caravan, Ballet Society, School of American Ballet
"New York City Ballet", 202
"The New York City Ballet", 69
The New York City Ballet, 57, 204
New York City Ballet [souvenir program, 1971], 200; [1975], 206
New York City Ballet: A Gala Performance . . . May 12, 1976, 213
New York City Ballet: Hommage à Ravel, 1875–1975, 187, 207
New York City Ballet: Igor Stravinsky . . . 1882– . . . 1971, 201
New York City Ballet: Photographs . . . by George Platt Lynes, 189
The New York City Ballet Guild Presents . . . the School of American Ballet, 209
The New York City Ballet 1946–1971 (1934–1980), 199
New York City Opera, 371
New York *Evening Journal*, 95
New York *Herald Tribune*, 96, 99, 369, 381
New York Letter", 442

New York Review of Books, 201
New York State Theater, 192
New York State Theater Magazine, 193, 194, 198, 203
New York *Times*, 92, 162, 174, 299, 337, 384
"Newbold Morris", 471
"Newell Convers Wyeth", 327
Newhall, Beaumont, 331, 332, 338
Newhall, Nancy, 338
"The News Reels", 346
Nicolson, Sir Harold, 454
Nijinska, Bronislava, 88
Nijinsky, Romola de Pulszky, 48, 82
Nijinsky, Vaslav, 48, 59, 82, 88, 131, 148, 172
"Nijinsky", 82
Nijinsky, 48, 82
Nijinsky Dancing, 59
"1948–1975", 206
"1934–1959", 191
"1933–1944", 186
Noguchi, Isamu, 94
Norman, Dorothy, 458
North American Review, 100
The Norton Anthology of Modern Poetry, 24, 31
"Not Three Weeks", 235
"A Note on the Photographer", 333
"Notes for an Ingenious Freshman", 398
"Notes on Painting", 239
"Nothing at All", 8
Notre Dame des Cadres, 10
Nourissier, François, 339
Novack, George, 429

'The Nutcracker', 71, 188
The Nutcracker, 188
The Nutcracker: The Story . . . , 71

O'Brien, Edward J., 445
Ocampo, Victoria, 459
"The Occasion", 201
O'Clair, Robert, 31, 32
Odyssey, 439
O'Faoláin, Seán, 411
Oliver, María Rosa, 318, 459
"On Choreography", 198
"On Producing 'A Midsummer Night's Dream'", 365
"On Stravinsky", 201
O'Neill, Eugene Gladstone, 366
Original Ballet Russe, 78, 106, 132, 134, 138, 140
'Orpheus', 201
"Our Ballet and Our Audience", 115
"Our Dancers' Debt", 190
Ouroussow, Evgenia: *see* Lehovich, Evgenia Ouroussow

PM's Weekly, 138
'Paganini', 138
Palmer, Winthrop, 66
"Paris Alive", 462
Parker, Dorothy, 445
Parnassus, 240
'Le Pas d'Acier', 75
"Pas de Deux in 2 x 4", 124
Pasley, Fred D., 403
"Pavel Tchelitchew", 324
Pavel Tchelitchew: An Exhibition, 324

"Pavel Tchelitchew: An Unfashionable Painter", 294
Pavel Tchelitchew: Pinturas y Dibujos, 318
Pavel Tchelitchew Drawings, 221
Pavlova, Anna, 77, 150
"Pedro Figari", 259
Pedro Figari, 1861–1938, 259
Pendleton, Ralph, 380
"Permanence and the Present", 448
"The Persistence of Ballet", 80
Perspectives USA, 166
Petipa, Marius, 157
'Petrouchka', 174
"Philip Reisman", 238
Phillips Exeter Monthly, 4
Photographs by Cartier-Bresson, 332
"Photographs of America", 330
The Photographs of Henri Cartier-Bresson, 331
"Photography", 335
"Photography in the United States", 329
Photography 1930, 305
Picasso, Pablo, 94, 260, 261, 263, 302
Picasso and the Ballet, 261
"Pictures from an Album", 377
"The Plastic Arts", 268
Playbill, 71, 178, 190, 193, 194, 204, 205, 210, 212–215
Pocahontas, 38
"Poet and Prophet", 460
"Poets under Fire", 457
"The Policy of a Ballet Company", 210
Pollack, Peter, 338

"Popular Style in American Dancing", 112

Portinari, Candido, 251

"Portraits and Popular Myths", 250

"The Position of Balanchine", 166

"The Position of Pavel Tchelitchew", 243

Post-Caviar . . . , 364

"Postscript: Wystan at War", 30, 389

Pound, Ezra Loomis, 397

Powell, Eleanor, 112

"Prejudice Purely", 83

"Presence de France", 465

Print Review, 300

"A Prison of Possibility", 472

'Prodigal Son', 176

"Progress of M. Balanchine . . .", 95

Prokofiev, Serge, 75

"Public Mask and Private Sorrows", 270

"Purity through the Will", 382

Putnam, Howard Phelps, 394

"A Quasi-Preface", 319

Que Viva Méjico!, 353

"The Quest of the Golden Lamb", 254

Rachmaninov, Sergei, 138

Rackham, Arthur, 288

Rain, Charles, 39

"Rationale of a Repertory", 73

Der Raub der Mona Lisa, 351

Ravel, Maurice, 46, 187, 207

Ray, Man, 335, 347

Raynal, Maurice, 231

"Recent Latin American Novels", 461

"La Reciente Obra Mural de Siqueiros . . . ", 247

"Recollections", 204

"Record and Augury", 132

The Red Commander's Bride, 349

Redgrave, Vanessa, 363

"The Rediscovery of William Rimmer", 262

Reisman, Philip, 238

Reisz, Karel, 363

"Rembrandt and the Bankers", 290

Rembrandt van Rijn, 260, 290

Renaud, Madeleine, 349

"Repertory: Ballet Director Suggests . . . ", 162

"Repertory: Policy for the Repeatable", 371

"Repertory: The Face of the Company", 164

Repertory in Review, 73

"Report of the Director . . . 1941", 184; " . . . 1942", 185

"The Republic of Silence", 462

"Return Ticket Paid", 18

"Revolutionary Ballet Forms", 88

Reynolds, Nancy, 73

Rhymes and More Rhymes of a PFC, 13, 31

Rhymes of a PFC, 12, 13, 22–25, 31, 32

Rich, Daniel Catton, 319

Richard Benson, 344

Riggs, Lynn, 347
Rimmer, William, 229, 255, 258, 262, 315
"Rimmer, William", 229
"Rimmer Material", 255
Ripley, Katharine, 405
Rish, Sepp, 350
Rittman, Trude, 42
Rivière, Jacques, 59
The Road to Life, 345
Robbins, Jerome, 169
Robinson, Bill, 81
Rockefeller Center, 237, 442
Rogers, Ginger, 112
Rogge, Florence, 81
Romance Sentimentale, 351
The Romantic Ballet in London, 149
Roosen, L., 59
Rosenfeld, Alvin Hirsch, 387
Ross, Nancy Wilson, 467
"Roughrider, Muckraker, Gangster", 403
Roxyettes, 81
"Russian Ballet . . . ", 140
Ryan, Grace L., 122

Sachs, Curt, 110
"Sad but Hopeful", 105
Sage, Robert, 399
St. Armand, Barton Levi, 387
St. Denis, Ruth, 93
Saint-Gaudens, Augustus, 214, 225
Salmagundi, 166
Salus, Peter H., 30
Santa Cruz, Domingo, 147
Saratoga Performing Arts Center, 196

Saratoga Performing Arts Center: Saratoga Festival 1976, 213
The Saratoga Performing Arts Center Program Magazine, 196
Sartre, Jean-Paul, 462
Saturday Review of Literature, 443
Scarlatti, Domenico, 37
"Scenery for Theatrical Dancing", 94
"Das Schloss", 23, 31
Schoenberg, Bessie, 110
School of American Ballet, 35, 79, 80, 88, 92, 103, 184–186, 191, 197, 205, 208, 209, 211, 215
"The School of American Ballet", 215
The School of American Ballet [catalogue, 1941/1942], 184; [Fall/Winter 1942/1943], 185; [1944/1945], 186; [1959/1960], 191; [1970/1971], 197; [1976/1977], 211; [prospectus, 1937?], 103
"The School of American Ballet: 1934–1970", 197
"The School of American Ballet: 1934–1976", 211
School of American Ballet Tenth Annual Workshop Performances, 208
"The School of the American Ballet", 79
Schurz, Carl, 413
Schwann-1 Record & Tape Guide, 178
Schwarz, Boris, 384

Schwezoff, Igor, 96
"The Scope of Photography",
 338
The Sculpture of Elie Nadelman,
 317
The Sculpture of Gaston Lachaise,
 309
"Seeing Things . . . ", 260
Segall, Lasar, 251
Seldes, Gilbert, 420
Seurat, Georges, 260
Sewanee Review, 465
Shakespeare, William, 365, 366,
 374, 383
"Shakespeare and the Theatre of
 Style", 374
"Shakespeare Festival Theater",
 375
Shakespeare Quarterly, 293
Shan-Kar, Uday, 442
Shaw, Robert Gould, 225
"Sheer Miracle to the Multi-
 tude'", 298
Shenandoah, 30
Show, 294
"Siegfriedslage", 30, 389
Siegmeister, Elie, 62
The Silver Fan," 4
Simon, Michel, 349
Simonson, Lee, 75, 368
Siqueiros, David, 247–249
Siqueiros: Painter and Revolu-
 tionary", 249
Siqueiros in Chillán", 248
Sisson, Charles Jasper, 365
Sitting Bull, 432
Sitting Bull Good Charac-
 ter . . . ", 432
Slonimsky, Yury, 157

Smith, W. Eugene, 334
Snake Hips, 81
"Some American Dancers", 89
"South American Painting", 251
Speer, Albert, 472
The Spellbound Child, 46, 187
Spender, Stephen, 30, 389, 452
Spokane [Washington] *Spokes-
 man-Review,* 170
"Stardom: Slav and Native", 114
"The State of Modern Painting",
 267
Steffens, Lincoln, 403
Stieglitz, Alfred, 335
"The Stepchild of the Arts", 99
Storrs, Sir Ronald, 453
"Stratford on Another Avon",
 372
Stratford, Ontario, Shakespeare
 Festival, 372, 379
Strauss, Johann, 36
Stravinsky, Igor, 101, 102, 158,
 174, 200, 201, 377, 378, 382
"Stravinsky and Balanchine", 200
The Stravinsky Festival . . . , 201
Stravinsky in the Theatre, 101
Strawbridge, Edwin, 75
Streicher, Julius, 464
Stuart, J. E. B., 423
Stuart, Muriel, 65
Studio, 251
"A Subscription Audience for
 Ballet", 194
Sullivan, Mark, 436
Suzuki, Daisetz T., 466
"The Swell Guy", 394
Swope, Martha, 53, 57, 60, 71,
 72, 201
'Les Sylphides', 49

"Symbol and Device", 273
Symbolic Realism, 320
Symbolic Realism in American Painting, 322

TAC Magazine, 124, 357
" 'T. E. "Lawrence" ' ", 446
Taggard, Genevieve, 21
Tamiris, Helen, 89
Taras, John, 47
'Tarzan', 350
The Taste of Napoleon, 326
Taylor, Paul B., 30
Tchelitchew, Pavel, 94, 221, 243, 265, 294, 318, 324
Ten Introductions, 19, 21
Thayr, Forrest, Jr., 43
Theatre Arts Committee, 357
Theatre Arts, 91, 131, 132, 136, 147, 158, 159, 168
Theatre Arts Anthology, 158
"Theatre Chronicle", 366
Theatregoer, 202
"This Month in the Dance" [column], 140, 141
Thoby-Marcelin, Philippe, 461
Thomason, John W., 423
Thompson, Oscar, 62
Thomson, Virgil, 40
"Those Remarkable Russians", 364
Three Pamphlets Collected, 51–53, 55
"Threesome", 24
Time Table, 45
Times Literary Supplement, 169, 173
"To Dance", 108

"To Do Again", 168
To Honor Henry McBride, 319
"To the Editors", 130
"To Yell with Hale", 402
Tolstoy, Leo, 362, 427
Town & Country, 108, 134, 246, 254, 459
Transcendence, 35
"Transcontinental Caravan", 119
transition, 399
Trotsky, Leon, 406, 418
"Trotsky Puts Russia in New Light", 406
Tudor, Antony, 45
"Tudoresque", 25
Tunney, Gene, 433
Twelve Sculptors, 311
Twice a Year, 458
"Tyranny and Blackmail", 107
Tyrone Guthrie Theatre, 383

"U.N.", 26
U.S. Camera, 338
'Union Jack', 60, 213
"Union Jack", 213
Union Jack, 60
'Union Pacific', 86
"The United States of Henri Cartier-Bresson", 342
University of Pennsylvania Museum Bulletin, 280
University of Virginia, 444

Valéry, Paul, 465
Van Praagh, Peggy, 173
Van Vechten, Carl, 470
"Vaudeville", 24, 31, 32

Vecheslova, Tatiana, 80
Vestal, Stanley, 432
View, 243
Villa, José Garcia, 445
Villiers, Alan J., 405
"Virginia Letter", 444
Virginia Quarterly Review, 445
"A Visit to Der Stuermer", 464
"A Visit to Manuel de Falla",
  369
Vogue, 78, 175
Voices, 187

W. Eugene Smith, 334
W.H. Auden: A Tribute, 30, 389
Walker Evans, 330
"Walt Whitman & Thomas
  Eakins . . . ", 340
"War and Peace", 362
War and Peace, 362, 427
"War Uncovers a Ghost of Goth-
  ic Fresco", 253
Watkins, Franklin, 35, 239
Watteau, Jean Antoine, 260
Watts, Alan W., 466
"The Wealth of the Orient", 292
Weidman, Charles, 81, 89
Weismuller, Johnny, 350
Weller, George Anthony, 443
Wells, H. G., 393
West, Buster, 112
"Western", 28
Weston, Edward, 335
The Wet Parade, 355
What Ballet Is about, 53, 55

"*What* (Who?) *Is* a Fire(?)
  Bird (?)?", 218
"What Will History Say of Picas-
  so", 263
White (photographer), 59
White House Happening, 33
Whitman, Walt, 340, 455
Wigman, Mary, 75, 77, 89
Wilde, John, 321
Wilder, Alec, 44
William Rimmer, 315
"William Rimmer: His Life and
  Art", 315
Winston, Clara and Richard,
  472
Winters, Yvor, 448
Wood, Grant, 241
"Working with Stravinsky", 101
World's Fair, Chicago, 1934,
  447
World's Fair, Seattle, 1962, 469
Wyeth, Betsy James, 297
Wyeth, James, 325
Wyeth, Newell Convers, 297,
  327

Yale University Library Gazette,
  470
Yankee Clipper, 39
"Yasuhide Kobashi", 328
Yates, Elizabeth Hall, 401

Ziegfeld Follies, 81
Zipser, Arthur, 429

EAKINS

Produced by the Eakins Press Foundation
for the Yale University Library

Designed by Howard I. Gralla

Composed and printed
by Michael and Winifred Bixler

Plates by The Meriden Gravure Company

Bound by Robert Burlen & Son